MERSEY MINIS

VOLUME FIVE

LEAVING

edited by

Deborah Mulhearn

GW00660443

Mersey Minis

VOLUME FIVE: LEAVING

Edited by Deborah Mulhearn
Illustrations by Clare Curtis
Graphic design by Ken Ashcroft
Printed and bound in Italy by Graphicom

ISBN: 978-0-9556547-1-8

First published in November 2007 by Capsica Ltd
83 Ampthill Road, Liverpool L17 9QN, UK

email: merseyminis@capsica.net
www.merseyminis.com
www.loveliverpoolbooks.com

CONTENTS

Dedicated to
Annette, Nick, Tom, Richard, Helena and Rachel

INTRODUCTION

LEAVING is the fifth and final volume of the Mersey Minis series. The five volumes, LANDING, LIVING, LONGING, LOVING and LEAVING, together present an 800th anniversary anthology of writing about Liverpool from its muddy beginnings to its future dreams.

LEAVING could have been filled with accounts of dock departures – millions sailed from Liverpool to a new life – but for the sake of variety I've broadened the theme to all modes of departure, with the Liverpool of imagination and memory as well as literal leavings included. As the Liverpool-born jazz singer George Melly put it, 'The departure for the Sea of Dreams is from the Liverpool pierhead.'

From Pullitzer prize-winning authors to poor emigrants passing through Liverpool – and in some cases staying – these extracts are vivid and moving accounts of loss and exuberant reinvention.

Poorer travellers' experiences contrast sharply with the comforts of the well heeled, the privations of the boarding house against the luxuries of the Adelphi. Some get glimpses into this gilded world, like the acerbic lady's maid unimpressed by the hotel's French menu.

Others left by road and rail. A famous poet takes the coach called the 'Lousy Liverpool' and is bitten by fleas and pickpockets; an early rail traveller is traumatised when an oncoming train rushes past (at 35 mph) on the adjacent track.

People are leaving home, leaving childhood, leaving for the suburbs, leaving the known, leaving life. A young boy, now a celebrated horror writer, sees 'bird man' Leo Valentin plummet to his death at Speke Airport in 1956. A freed slave is afraid to leave his ship.

   Liverpool may have been merely a staging post for many, their last glimpse of England or Europe, but it's a place imprinted on the minds and memories of millions.

DEBORAH MULHEARN

A NOTE ON THE TEXT

The extracts in Mersey Minis are reproduced from original sources, many of which are historic and therefore sometimes using styles and language unfamiliar to modern readers. I have, however, in most cases retained the original spellings, punctuation and sometimes the grammatical mistakes so as not to impede the energy and flow of the writer, and to reflect the uniqueness and idiosyncracy of his or her account.

   The date given at the start of each extract is the date the writing refers to, and not necessarily when it was written or published. For publication dates and further details please see the book list on p108.

LEAVING

Jonathan Raban 1988

There is a sentence that has stirred the imagination of Europe as powerfully as any call to arms. I've seen it written a hundred times, and have always felt a pang of envy for its lucky author. It is so jaunty, so unreasonably larger than life. It promises to deliver the unexpected – some fantastic reversal of fortune, some miraculous transfiguration in the character of the writer. It deserves a paragraph to itself, and should be printed in ceremonious italics.

Having arrived in Liverpool, I took ship for the New World.

Behind the sentence crowd the emigrants themselves – a crew of people dingy enough to take a little of the shine out of the words. They stand in line: the long-out-of-work, the illiterate, the chronically drunk, the hapless optimists, the draft-dodgers, the bankrupt adventurers. Some, like the Jews escaping the Pale of the Tsars, are dignified by the involuntary heroism that attaches itself to any persecuted people; but most of the single men and families on the dock are not – were not – refugees. If they were on the run, they were more likely to be fleeing tallymen and creditors than cruel kings and despots.

*****

The Old World was in bad shape. It was coming down around my ears as I drove north out of the city through the Victorian docks that line the Mersey. At least they had been docks. Now they were smoking heaps of brickdust. I drove through an orange fog of dust. Dust caked the windshield of the car. Even from behind closed windows, one could taste the dust, its mouldy sweetness, like stale cooked liver. Ball-swinging cranes stood idle in the muggy afternoon  heat. Raised over the dustheaps were the yellow Portakabins of the demolition contractors, on tall stilts of scaffolding.

'The last of England ...' I said.

My wife said nothing. She'd imagined a more romantic maritime setting to say goodbye in, and I could see it too... worn paving stones, old iron bollards, trapdoor warehouses with cantilevered blocks and tackles. The swinging balls had demolished everything, including our goodbyes.

Every so often there was a gap between the ruins and the improbable glimpse of a ship. I saw the listless flags of Japan, Liberia and Greece, but no British ensign. Most of the British mercantile fleet had been either scrapped or 'reflagged' – registered in Liberia, or the Isle of Man, or some other country where taxes were low and shipping regulations easygoing. In the last ten years the 'red duster' had turned into a nostalgic rarity, and there was none on view among the dustheaps, where a duster of any colour would have been welcome.

In the middle of the waste land, the demolition men had

left behind a sailors' pub whose scrolled Edwardian stuccowork lent an ironic touch of mouldering finery to this devastated place. I parked the car on a patch of cinders and we crossed the dual carriageway to the pub. Inside, the flavour of brickdust was seasoned wih the eye-watering tang of Old Holborn cigarette tobacco. We sat side by side on a wooden bench holding glasses of Spanish brandy.

'Cheers,' my wife said cheerlessly.

After ten silent minutes of pretending an exaggerated interest in the sluggish movement of the coloured balls around the pool table, I said, 'I suppose we'd better find my ship.' The Old Holborn in the air seemed to have got the better of my wife's eyes.

The ship was easy to find. At what had once been Seaforth it towered over the dustheaps, in wedding-cake tiers, topped by a spinney of radar scanners. Its name, *Atlantic Conveyor*, was clear from half a mile away, and it was flying a Red Ensign the size of an embroidered wall-hanging. Between us and it lay a shantytown of steel containers with mobile gantries and forklift trucks plying in the streets, a mile or so of 20-foot-high chainlink fencing and a Portakabin guardhouse in which a bored attendant was staring at *The Sun*.

My wife and I embraced wanly. I lugged my bags from the boot of the car to the guardhouse, and watched the car lumber and sway over the potholes in the tarmac and disappear into the orange fog of the Waterloo Road. It was not the dockside farewell that either of us had planned. Proper farewells need a suitable architecture on which to stage them. Kissing was not an activity that was catered for by the bald amenities of the Seaforth Container Terminal.

Noam Chomsky 2004

Liverpool occupies a special place in my memories.

Thomas Clarkson 1808

The temper of many of the interested people of Liverpool had now become still more irritable, and their hostility more apparent than before. I received anonymous letters, entreating me to leave it, or I should otherwise never leave it alive. The only effect, which this advice had upon me, was to make me more vigilant when I went out at night. I never stirred out at this time without Mr. Falconbridge. And he never accompanied me without being well armed. Of this, however, I knew nothing until we had left the place. There was certainly a time, when I had reason to believe that I had a narrow escape. I was one day on the pier-head with many others looking at some little boats below at the time of a heavy gale. Several persons, probably out of curiosity, were hastening thither. I had seen all I intended to see, and was departing, when I noticed eight or nine persons making towards me. I was then only about eight or nine yards from the precipice of the pier, but going from it. I expected that they would have divided to let me through them; instead of which they closed upon me and bore me back. I was borne within a yard of the precipice, when I discovered my danger; and perceiving among them the murderer of Peter Green, and two others who had insulted me at the King's Arms, it instantly struck me that they had a design to throw me over the pier-head; which they might have done at this time, and yet have pleaded that I had been killed by accident. There was not a moment to lose. Vigorous on account of the danger, I darted forward. One of them, against whom I pushed myself, fell down. Their ranks were broken. And I escaped, not without blows, amidst their imprecations and abuse.

Rosaria Crolla   2007

Leaving my beloved home in Glasgow, to live and run a business in Liverpool, I felt like those 19th century Italians who so reluctantly left their homeland in search of ecomomic stability and who were faced with a city like no other in Europe, in my opinion. Liverpool is a haven for everything different, independent and anyone can call this home.

Reverend Francis Kilvert   1872

Thursday, 20 June
At ten o'clock Mr, Mrs, Miss Gwatkin and I went down to the Landing Stage and embarked on board a steamboat for New Brighton on the Cheshire side of the Mersey, a suburb· of

Birkenhead. The morning was lovely, all was fresh and new, the salt air and the wind exhilarating and I was in dancing spirits. The Mersey was gay and almost crowded with vessels of all sorts moving up and down the river, ships, barques, brigs, brigantines, schooners, cutters, colliers, tugs, steamboats, lighters, 'flats', everything from the huge emigrant liner steamship with four masts to the tiny sailing and rowing boat. From the river one sees to advantage the miles of docks which line the Mersey side, and the forests of masts which crowd the quays, 'the pine forest of the sea, mast and spar'.

At New Brighton there are beautiful sands stretching for miles along the coast and the woods wave green down to the salt water's edge. The sands were covered with middle class Liverpool folks and children out for a holiday, digging in the sand, riding on horses and donkeys, having their photographs taken, and enjoying themselves generally. Some of the lady and gentlemen riders upon the hired horses were pitiable objects, bumping up and down upon their saddles like flour sacks, and even requiring their horses to be led for them. The ladies as a rule rode without riding habits and with crinolines. The effect was striking.

As we came down the river this morning several large emigrant ships lay in the river getting up steam and the Blue Peter, the signal for sailing, flying at the fore. They were going down the river this afternoon. They seemed crowded with Irish and German emigrants and small steam-boats kept bringing fresh loads of passengers alongside the big ships. One could not help thinking of the hundreds of sorrowful hearts on board and ashore and the farewells and partings for ever, so many of them, on this side of the grave.

George Melly 1969

The departure for 'the Sea of Dreams' is from the Liverpool pierhead.

Henry Theodore Tuckerman 1852

It is a singular fact, that the busy scenes, and palpable results of traffic, and the melancholy quietude of death, are the two points of reflective interest in Liverpool; her docks and her cemeteries, are the principal attractions. Nothing in her prosperous mart serves to remind us that the inhabitants petitioned Elizabeth for exemption of taxes on account of poverty – that Prince Rupert besieged the city in 1644, or that the monks once had a monopoly of the Birkenhead ferry; but, looking through the iron railing down into St James' cemetery, we see the monument of Huskisson, a stone memorial erected by the sea-captains to their shipwrecked brother, surrounded by evergreens – and recognise the fact, that the wealth which has here found a nucleus, was derived from maritime and commerical enterprise. It is a remarkable coincidence, that the basis of Liverpool's importance was the slave-trade, and that by a natural reaction, her citizens were among the most efficient advocates of its legal prohibition.

The city has a pleasant rural vicinage, and a ride among the hedges and villas, besides cheering the eye in winter, with many a picturesque lodge embowered in holly and graceful hayricks planted on the greenest sward, and, in

summer, alive with flowers, and musical with birds – warms the fancy with the view of Allerton Hall, the tasteful abode of Roscoe, and Wavertree so long the home of Mrs Hemans. Well may a poet, however, despair of catching even a glimpse of his traveller's castle in the air, while at Liverpool. He treads the dank pavement of Lord street, and looks around on the panorama of stores, cotton, beer, and coal drays, policemen with glossy hats, flying cabs, sailors arrayed for a holyday, thrusting out their boots to be polished with a comical air of reckless self-importance; he winds his perilous track along the river-side, where a wilderness of rigging is painted on a vast background of fog, a black steam-tug meanders through a forest of hulls and spars, hordes of poor emigrants are collecting their household utensils for a voyage, or gangs of muscular draymen are smoking black pipes – amid the clatter of wheels, hoofs, oaths, mariner's songs, and huckster's cries; he dines with a hospitable merchant, and is environed only with all the means and appliances of prosaic comfort; he returns to the Adelphi or the Waterloo, to meet an English sportsman, fresh from the Baltic or Europa, just landing in the hall a champagne-basket full of prairie birds; and he enters the coffee-room to behold the complacent mercantile effigies round the wall, the same old half-excavated Stilton, and a fresh New York journal on the table.

What room is there for retrospection, when steam and electricity thus concentrate the significance of every passing hour, and the products of sea-divided countries? How is it possible to attain any sense of the past when the present is thus omniverous; and what is there in the life and environment of Liverpool to divert the mind an instant from the actual and material to-day? How shall we flit from the new to the old, from modern, commercial, everyday England, to that which we have learned to love through Shakespere? Take the railway for Chester.

Ray Gosling 1958

Liverpool: Good Friday, 1958 – the city of ships, the port – that grisly reminder that from Liverpool one sails for darkest Africa, South America, and that land of the free on the other side of the ocean. Liverpool: sailors and dockers: grim, grisly, dirty, grimy, stealing, screaming, wide and winding like the Mersey from the oil plants down by the Cast Iron Shore, the Promenade at Aigburth, the holes in the wall, the Dingle, the hole in the ground where the overhead railway has been ripped away, Pier Head, and the passenger docks down to Gladstone, and Pier Head. Pier Head – the green dirty buses to Litherland and Speke – the converging streets, Rodney, Nelson, Pitt, Grafton, Hope, Paradise, Pier Head; your last glimpse of England.

William Camden 1582

From Warrington, the Mersey grows broader, and soon after contracts again; but it at last opens into a wide mouth very commodious for trade, and then runs into the sea near Liverpool, in Saxon Lifer-pole, commonly Lirpool; so called (as it is thought) from the water spread there like a fen. It is the most convenient and usual place for setting sail into Ireland, but not so eminent for antiquity, as for neatness and populousness.

Janet Smith

1896

Left the Central Station at 10 o'clock & the train went at such a rate we were being thrown from side to side I was quite glad when we arrived Exchange Station which we did shortly after three. there was a large bus meeting us & drove us right up to the Adelphi Hotel. it is a very large hotel & is managed splendidly. All the corredors are solid white marble – after getting a wash down we went down to the drawing room then at 6 o'clock we went into dinner. Mrs M – says to me just order what you want, all very well when all the menu's were in French I left that dining room I went to another one the English dining room & asked for the standard dish ham & eggs & tea. I enjoyed it very much

Reverend James Shaw

1854

The crew were stout looking men, weather beaten sons of Neptune, the officers were sufficiently imperious in their orders to them. Captain Ferbur, the commander, was a portly looking gentleman, who gave his orders from the quarter deck through his officers to his men. The passengers were of different nationalities. There were some two hundred Irish emigrants, full of fun and frolic. There were a few loquacious French, polished and refined in manner. There was a large number of Germans, serious and solemn in appearance. There were a few short-necked, broad-shouldered Dutch, as if the dams of Holland had been carried on their heads. There were Swiss from Switzerland, Italians from Italy, and Jews from different parts of the world. There were some Yorkshire farmers, and miners from Cornwall, who talked as our forefathers did three hundred years ago. Beside these, there were merchants from London and Manchester, and a goodly number of Scotch from Scotland, and Welch from Wales. The trades had a variety of representatives, so had the religious  denominations. There were Roman Catholics, Episcopalians, Methodists, and Presbyterians, Baptists, Jews, Quakers, and Lutherans. Some who were true believers, and others who believed in nothing but folly. There were Deists, Pantheists, and Atheists; some who did not believe in a God, and some who believed that God was everything, and everything was God. With many of these I had subsequently to contend in controversy for the 'Faith once delivered to the saints.'

The evening was fine, the sails were unfurled, the anchor weighed, and the steam tug drew us out to open sea for America. Passengers on deck waved adieus to friends on shore, while the sails, filled with the rising breeze, bore the vessel onward after the steamer. The voice of weeping passengers were hushed by the loud wild songs of the sailors, as they pulled the ropes or climbed the masts.

Helen Pitsillos

My mum and dad had left their family home in Larnaca, Cyprus, to begin a new life in Liverpool. They bought a café in Lodge Lane and called it the 'Knife and Fork' Café, (the customers often joked that it was a good job it wasn't the other way round). Being a Greek teenager in the midst of Scousers was a strange experience at times, but life in Toxteth was about to get a lot more interesting in the summer of 1981.

I remember it as being the year that Prince Charles and Lady Diana got married. A large cake, with the happy couple made in icing, copied from the official engagement photograph, was displayed in the shop window next door to our café. For some reason this image has always stuck in my memory. One day at the beginning of July, I was playing with my siblings in the living room of our house above the café. It was around teatime and still light. At the sound of smashing glass and screaming, I looked down into the street from the window. There was smoke and flames coming from the chemist over the road. Lodge Lane was teeming with people. They were running up the lane, and running down the lane, shouting, shoving, screeching, with armfuls of items like jeans and shoes. Some were pushing trolleys from the Kwik Save, overflowing with food. One woman was wheeling a hoover down the road. Another man threw a pair of shoes up into the air, shouting 'these aren't my size!' I couldn't understand the mayhem outside, but knew things were going to get a lot more hectic. My nine-year old brother put a saucepan on his head, saying 'this will make a good helmet.'

I thought I'd better go and find my mum and dad, but before I knew it my dad had all four of us kids lined up outside the café; and there we stood fast against the looters, protecting our little Greek empire. The Toxteth Riots had begun. The police were nowhere to be seen. We stood and watched for what seemed like hours. At one point I saw my history teacher, who lived over the road, who said he didn't think I'd be going to school for a few days. It would have been difficult, as the Chemist's had just blown up and was blocking the road, and the bus stop had disappeared beneath the rubble.

The sweet shop two doors away was raided and set alight. The Asian man who lived above it was quickly carried out over the shoulders of a fireman. At the time I didn't feel scared, I had no sense of fear, just fascination, even when a man came up to me and, pointing at the café, said 'You're next!'

Three men broke into Stanley Racing, the betting shop next door, and reappeared carrying a huge safe. Despite their best efforts, they couldn't get it open. They even shouted over to my dad, 'have you got a hammer, mate?' My dad looked at them in disbelief and said, in his strong Greek accent, 'No, mate I haven't'. In the end they gave up and left it in the middle of the street.

Although all this happened twenty six years ago, it's still vivid in my mind. Lodge Lane has changed. Before the Toxteth Riots it was a thriving, vibrant and safe community full of bubbly personalities. Our café is now part of Stanley Racing, who obviously recovered from the loss of their safe. The window that I looked out of is still boarded up. No-one has lived there since we left.

April Ashley 1950

I decided to take myself in hand. I recognised that it was no good wanting to be a girl. I would be a man. When nobody was around I croaked away in the lower registers until my voice was forcibly broken or at least roughened up. I couldn't speak

for five days and the local Indian doctor told Mother I had 'done something mental' to my voice. More important, I made the decision to go to sea. All the other men in my family had gone to sea, even little Ivor, my brother. The sea seemed to be one of the things that made you a man.

My grocery deliveries took me to the smartest districts of Liverpool. Since these were a long way from the town centre, I would be given cups of tea when I arrived. One of my favourite destinations was the house of Mrs Rossiter. To me she was a creature from outer space, with her elegant hair-dos, long manicured fingernails, Tradesmen's Entrance and sprinkler on the lawn. Mr Rossiter was an important man at the Cunard Shipping line and, when I confided to his wife my plan to go to sea, she arranged for him to interview me in the Cunard Building.

'But you are much too young to go to sea,' stated Mr Rossiter. I was fifteen but looked about eleven years old. 'But I'm not too young to go to training school, am I?' I replied. Mr Rossiter gave me a magnificent letter of introduction on embossed Cunard paper. It cut through all the red tape such as medical tests and parental consent, which was a boon because I had told none of my family or friends about my decision. I had not even told John and Edna who were the most important people in my life in case they raised obstructions.

The night before departure I came home from work and said, 'Mum, I'm leaving tomorrow to join a cadet ship.' 'Well, isn't that somethin',' she said, and finished cutting up a potato and tossed what were destined to be Bernie's chips into the chip pan.

On a damp November morning I stood at Lime Street Station with a small brown cardboard suitcase, waiting for the train to Bristol en route for the cadet ship SS *Vindicatrix*. My only personal memento were rosary beads. I was superstitious.

The training course was intense and lasted six weeks. 'What are these, sir?' I asked looking at various samples of tied rope. 'Knots!' replied the instructor. 'What the bloody hell,' I thought. Knots. I never could do them. I did bows instead.

Thomas de Quincey

1802

Some few years before this event, a prodigious fire occurred at Liverpool: the Goree, a vast pile of warehouses close to one of the docks, was burned to the ground. The huge edifice, eight or nine storeys high, and laden with most combustible

 goods,– many thousand bales of cotton, wheat and oats in thousands of quarters, tar, turpentine, rum, gunpowder, &c.,– continued through many hours of darkness to feed this tremendous fire. To aggravate the calamity, it blew a regular gale of wind; luckily for the shipping, it blew inland,– that is, to the east; and all the way down to Warrington, eighteen miles distant to the eastward, the whole air was illuminated by flakes of cotton, often saturated with rum, and by what seemed absolute worlds of blazing sparks, that lighted up all the upper chambers of the air. All the cattle lying abroad in the fields through a breadth of eighteen miles were thrown into terror and agitation. Men, of course, read in this hurrying overhead of scintillating and blazing vortices the annunciation of some gigantic calamity going on in Liverpool; and the lamentation on that account was universal. But that mood of public sympathy did not at all interfere to suppress or even to check the momentary bursts of rapturous admiration, as this arrowy sleet of many-coloured fire rode on the wings of hurricane, alternately through open depths of air or through dark clouds overhead.

Fritz Spiegl   1999

The accent has also become less gutteral because people are healthier, the air is cleaner, there is less catarrh about and people smoke less. But there's no sign of it becoming estuary Scouse.

Isabella Bird   1854

Although bi-weekly steamers ply between England and the States, and many mercantile men cross the Atlantic twice annually on business, and think nothing of it, the voyage seems an important event when undertaken for the first time. Friends living in inland counties, and those who have been sea-sick in crossing the straits of Dover, exaggerate the dangers and discomforts of ocean travelling, and shake their heads knowingly about fogs and icebergs.

Then there are a certain number of boxes to be packed, and

a very uncertain number of things to fill them, while clothing has to be provided suitable to a tropical summer, and a winter within the arctic circle. But a variety of minor arrangements, and even an indefinite number of leave-takings, cannot be indefinitely prolonged; and at eight o'clock on a Saturday morning in 1854, I found myself with my friends on the landing-stage at Liverpool.

Whatever sentimental feelings one might be inclined to indulge in on leaving the shores of England were usefully and instantaneously annihilated by the discomfort and crush in the *Satellite* steam-tender, in which the passengers were conveyed, helplessly huddled together like a flock of sheep, to the *Canada*, an 1850-ton paddle-wheel steamer of the Cunard line, which was moored in the centre of the Mersey.

An investigation into the state-rooms, and the recital of disappointed expectations consequent on the discovery of their very small dimensions, the rescue of 'regulation' portmanteaus from sailors who were running off with them, and the indulgence of that errant curiosity which glances at everything and rests on nothing, occupied the time before the arrival of the mail-boat with about two tons of letters and newspapers, which were consigned to the mail-room with incredible rapidity.

Then friends were abruptly dismissed – two guns were fired – the lashings were cast off – the stars and stripes flaunted gaily from the 'fore – the captain and pilot took their places on the paddle-boxes – the bell rang – our huge paddle-wheels revolved, and, to use the words in which the same event was chronicled by the daily press, 'The Cunard royal mail steamer *Canada*, Captain Stone, left the Mersey this morning for Boston and Halifax, conveying the usual mails; with one hundred and sixty-eight passengers, and a large cargo on freight.'

It was an auspiciously commenced voyage as far as appearances went. The summer sun shone brightly – the waves of the Mersey were crisp and foam-capped – and the fields of England had never worn a brighter green.

William Dean Howells   1909

The place was a little America which swelled into a larger with the arrivals of the successive steamers, though the soft swift English trains bore our co-nationals away as rapidly as they could. Many familiar accents remained till the morning, and the breakfast-room was full of a nasal resonance which would have made one at home anywhere in our East or West. I, who was then vainly trying to be English, escaped to the congenial top of the farthest bound tram, and flew, at the rate of four miles an hour, to the uttermost suburbs of Liverpool, whither no rumor of my native speech could penetrate. It was some balm to my wounded pride of country to note how pale and small the average type of the local people was. The poorer  classes swarmed along a great part of the tram-line in side streets of a hard, stony look, and what characterized itself to me as a sort of iron squalor seemed to prevail. You cannot anywhere have great prosperity without great adversity, just as you cannot have day without night, and the more Liverpool evidently flourished the more it plainly languished. I found no pleasure in the paradox, and I was not overjoyed by the inevitable ugliness of the brick villas of the suburbs into which these obdurate streets decayed. But then, after divers tram changes, came the consolation of beautiful riverside beaches, thronged with people who looked gay at that distance, and beyond the Mersey rose the Welsh hills, blue, blue.

Herman Melville   1839

The dead-house reminds me of other sad things; for in the vicinity of the docks are many very painful sights.

In going to our boarding-house, the sign of the Baltimore Clipper, I generally passed through a narrow street called 'Launcelott's-Hey,' lined with dingy, prison-like cotton warehouses. In this street, or rather alley, you seldom see any one but a truck-man, or some solitary old warehouse-keeper, haunting his smoky den like a ghost.

Once, passing through this place, I heard a feeble wail, which seemed to come out of the earth. It was but a strip of crooked side-walk where I stood; the dingy wall was on every side, converting the mid-day into twilight; and not a soul was in sight. I started, and could almost have run, when I heard that dismal sound. It seemed the low, hopeless, endless wail of some one forever lost. At last I advanced to an opening which communicated downward with deep tiers of cellars beneath a crumbling old warehouse; and there, some fifteen feet below the walk, crouching in nameless squalor, with her head bowed over, was the figure of what had been a woman. Her blue arms folded to her livid bosom two shrunken things like children, that leaned toward her, one on each side. At first, I knew not whether they were alive or dead. They made no sign; they did not move or stir; but from the vault came that soul-sickening wail.

I made a noise with my foot, which, in the silence, echoed far and near; but there was no response. Louder still; when one of the children lifted its head, and cast upward a faint glance; then closed its eyes, and lay motionless. The woman also, now gazed up, and perceived me; but let fall her eye again. They were dumb and next to dead with want. How they had crawled into that den, I could not tell; but there they had crawled to die. At that moment I never thought of relieving them; for death was so stamped in their glazed and unimploring eyes, that I almost regarded them as already no more. I stood looking down on them, while my whole soul swelled within me; and I asked myself, What right had any body in the wide world to smile and be glad, when sights like this were to be seen? It was enough to turn the heart to gall; and make a man-hater of a Howard. For who were these ghosts that I saw? Were they not human beings? A woman and two girls? With eyes, and lips, and ears like any queen? with hearts which, though they did not bound with blood, yet beat with a dull, dead ache that was their life.

Dirk Pieter Van den Bergh   1906

Anger and disappointment tighten up our throats. Shall we really leave, after all? Why did we have to be ready at the ungodly early hour of 4 o'clock? These questions were not answered. The directors and management do what they will and we have no way to defend ourselves. The children stand sleeping against the tables. So, impatient and frustrated, we are waiting and cursing the Dominion Line and all who are connected with it until 11 o'clock am. Finally there appears a big carriage. The street is crowded with emigrants, among which are some that were not from our hotel group. In the usual slow and easy-going manner, the passengers, (right now, the most of them Polish Jews) are packed as herrings in a barrel – into the carriage, baggage and all. From some other companies I noticed they had separate freight wagons for the baggage. Four more carriages follow. With craning necks we stand listening if they will call us, but none came. For the 5th carriage they called Julius Meyer, Joseph Stepp and the two Russian lady friends. All four had been guests at the same table with us. We shake our friends' hands now and bid them farewell. Julius Meyer, however, does not step in. Those who entered before him are so unkempt and filthy and smelly – so they let their turn go by; the carriage was plenty full anyway and rolled away. The sixth carriage rolled in place. The Belgians call and asked, when their turn is coming. 'Antwerp?' asked the agent. 'Yes,' they say. 'Come on,' was heard and the Belgians fly through the gates to pick up their baggage. I walk up to the man and shout: 'Can I go now, also?' on which he asked again, 'Antwerp?' I said 'yes' and again he said, 'come on' and away I was through the gate, to get our things and in two minutes we stepped into the carriage.

Edwin Chadwick   1842

Of the deaths which occurred amongst the labouring classes, it appears that no less than 62 per cent. of the total number were deaths under five years of age. Even amongst

those entered as shopkeepers and tradesmen, no less than 50 per cent. died before they attained that period. The proportion of mortality for Birmingham, where there are many insalubrious manufactories, but where the drainage of the town and the general condition of the inhabitants is comparatively good, was, in 1838, 1 in 40: whilst in Liverpool it was 1 in 31.

Richard Burton 1861

The day (August 24th, 186--) was a day to make the Englander leave England without a single sigh. A north of Europe nor'-wester had set in before noon, a funereal pall of rain-mist overhung the heavens of Liverpool with black, white sea-dogs coursed and worried one another over Father Mersey's breadth of mud, the shrewish gusts tore to pieces the very strongest showers–

Christopher Colbeck 1831

I at length got on board the Egremont Steamer which carries passengers to a ferry of that name the lowest down – on the Cheshire side there being two others one called Wood Side the other – to which the Steamers cross and recross every half hour. The sail occupied three quarters of an hour and was landed on paying 3d. which is the ferry price. From here I took a nice ramble to Perch Rock Battery which is about half a mile distant situate at the mouth of the Mersey built on an immense rock. I went all over and being perfectly new was a very pretty treat, guns being planted of an immense weight all round. Near to this is Black Rock Light-House which is built similar to Eddystone Light. I could not get to the top not having provided myself with a ticket. The view from here is very magnificent, the Steamers passing and repassing from Ireland, North Wales and Glasgow in great numbers and by the bye I might have gone from Liverpool to Dublin in the Best Cabin with provisions

and Stewards included for 7/6. Having enjoyed my ramble for some time a sailing boat hove in sight and having given the signal it put off to where I was, so running into a nice little bay I was enabled to jump on board and after a delightful sail landed at Liverpool and forthwith went to St Michael's Church and shortly afterwards entered St Luke's Church where having heard the sermon to its close I scrambled towards St George's Basin and there put off to the Floating Bath and had a fine bathe after which returned to Brunswick Street to dinner for which I was keenly prepared. Having made a hearty meal and drank a couple of glasses of wine I again sallied out and heard prayers at St George's Church and then having called and got my Baggage hastened to Lord St having booked my place for London that afternoon. The coach not being ready I again admired the Exchange which cost 30,000£ and was finished in 1749. At half past 4 we started from the Star Office Liverpool leaving this charming place with regret.

Fred Bower

In Liverpool, in 1904, I was working in Thornton's Yard, when the boss sent me to the Liverpool Cathedral site to shape a few stones. I was the first stone-cutter to cut a stone on the job. The present builders, Messrs. Morrison, were not on the job at that time. The work was let out, to be contracted for, in two sections, the foundations to the ground level, after which fresh tenders were called for, for the super-structure. This, I fancy, is a business dodge, the people who are having the work done knowing that contractors will cut prices on the first contract, in the hopes of getting the second, being on the ground with their tackle, and from the second contract recoup themselves for any losses on the first. Be that as it may, I was sent to the site. Here I met an old foreman whom I had worked under, on Eccleston church near Chester, for the old Duke of Westminster. He was Mr. Green, the first Clerk of Works on the job, and there till his death. We talked of old times, when two top-hatted men came forward and I sheered off and went on with my work. They were two of the committee men, one, I believe, Sir Frederick Radcliffe.

'Do you mind if I put a small souvenir', one said, 'down into the foundations?'

'Not at all,' replied the clerk.

And, gingerly, down the short ladder into the cavity where the old bricklayer, Sam Disley, was laying the blue Staffordshire bricks in a bed of cement and screened granite or limestone chippings, our friend stepped into the hole, some ten feet deep and twelve foot square, which was one of several that were filled with solid brickwork to the ground level, and were to carry the main columns of the cathedral.

The other man did the same, then they cleared off, whilst the Clerk of Works, knowing what men are, stood by watching, till a ton of bricks had been built over the place where the money had been inserted.

After he had gone, I thought 'I've as much right to be sentimental as them'. The only thing in the shape of a coin I possessed was a button. But that button had a history. In 1902 I had been in Canada. Walking along Yonge Street, Toronto's main thoroughfare, I saw a black object on the sidewalk. Picking it up, I found it was a button, seemingly stamped out of some hard composition, on which was impressed the words, 'Common Jails of Ontario'. I picked it up. In America most people carry a mascot. A coloured man generally has a rabbit's foot. An Irishman, a small dried potato 'to keep the rheumatics away', he will tell you. So I came by my mascot, and it was the mascot which followed the two gold coins, and now reposes in the cathedral foundations.

That night I had a further idea. As told, I had been

converted to Socialism, and was reading Blatchford's paper, the *Clarion*. The issues at that time were very trenchant with articles on 'Free Will', and attacks, or eulogies, on Blatchford's recent book, *God and my Neighbours*. So I hied myself off to a pal of mine with my idea. Here I may diverge.

In my youth at school, there were two exciting periods each year, when lessons were forgotten in a creed feud. Liverpool then, not so much now, was divided into two camps, Orangemen (perfervid Protestants) and Catholics. It was a common sight on St. Patrick's Day, or Orangeman's Day, July 12th, to see real gory battles between the sects. Each believed the only way to get to heaven was to send the other fellow to hell. The civic authorities were glad if these two days passed off each year without murder. And we school children had our battles. Near my school was a Catholic school, and their leader, at that time, was a tall, raw-boned Liverpool-born son of an Irishman. And somehow I was picked for the leader of our school. After school hours we would charge each other with sticks and stones. Sometimes we gave way, sometimes they. What with dodging the police, and the neighbours whose windows we were breaking, it was a great time. But, let that tall leader catch me by myself and I went through it. Two marks I will carry to the grave, where he cut my head open, or rather the skin that covers it.

It was not till 1912 that the venerable old agitator, Tom

Mann, came into the district, organized the workers, got the two factions together, and, with banners of intertwined orange and green, led a band through Liverpool composed of half-and-half Orangemen and Catholics, not playing 'To Hell with the Pope' or 'King William', but the brotherhood songs of the workers. However, to get back to the cathedral affair.

I visited my pal, the long, raw-boned boy, now a man, Jim Larkin, at his house. We who wanted to kill each other in our infantile ignorance had both joined the local Socialist Party and were the best of comrades. He got a piece of tin and compressed a copy each of the *Clarion* and the *Labour Leader* of June 24th, 1904, into it. I wrote the following short hurried note:

'To the Finders, Hail!'

'We, the wage slaves employed on the erection of this cathedral, to be dedicated to the worship of the unemployed Jewish carpenter, hail ye! Within a stone's throw from here, human beings are housed in slums not fit for swine. This message, written on trust-produced paper with trust-produced ink, is to tell ye how we of to-day are at the mercy of trusts. Building fabrics, clothing, food, fuel, transport, are all in the hands of money-mad, soul-destroying trusts. We can only sell our labour power, as wage slaves, on their terms. The money trusts to-day own us. In your own day, you will, thanks to the efforts of past and present agitators for economic freedom, own the trusts. Yours will indeed, compared to ours of to-day, be a happier existence. See to it, therefore, that ye, too, work for the betterment of all and so justify your existence by leaving the world the better for your having lived in it. Thus and thus only shall come about the Kingdom of 'God' or 'Good' on Earth. Hail, Comrades, and – Farewell.

Yours sincerely,
'A Wage Slave.'

This we put with the papers into the case, covered it with another sheet of tin, bent over the ends and edges to make it as air tight as possible, and, next day, I placed it in the foundations of the cathedral between two courses of bricks, and it was duly built in.

Carol Cochrane 1973

Our street is in a demolition area and dirt is everywhere. The smell of empty houses seeps through the streets. Cats limp into empty houses, and burrow themselves down for the night. Children rush into the houses and destroy the water pipes. The water starts to gush out and then the rats scatter. Oh, a sigh of relief when the workmen board up the houses, but still there aren't many left in our street. Never mind, our street is next on the list and it can't be long now.

Gerard Manley Hopkins   1881

Liverpool is of all places the most museless. It is indeed a most unhappy and miserable spot. There is moreover no time for writing anything serious – I should say composing it, for if it were made it might be written.

Virginia Woolf   1905

Reached Liverpool about 2.30 & went in a Bus to the pier, where a great many people were walking up & down, saying good bye, & preparing to go. A huge steamer, the *Oceanic*, 2nd largest afloat was black with passengers, just leaving for America. The *Anselm* came alongside in time, & we embarked. It is all white & clean & luxurious; we each have a cabin to ourself, in wh. I now write on my knees, & the sea is beginning to rise: We walked on the deck & saw all the lights along the Coast of Wales, steamers passing, & our own foam spread like white lace on the dark waters – a very lovely thing is a ship at sea.

Henry 'Starbuck' Perry   1874

We made the run to Liverpool with a general cargo from New York. After we got paid off I went on a drunk, and first thing I knew was when I woke up aboard of the Nova Scotia barque, and found that I'd been 'shanghaied,' and was on my way to Rio de Janeiro. 'Shanghai-ing' was common in them days. Some ships had a very bad name and had a hard time getting a crew. So the boarding-house masters used to fill a few men up with liquor and put them aboard a ship while they were drunk. By the time they came to, the vessel would be at anchor in midstream, or else towing out to sea.

Jules Verne 1867

The *Great Eastern* was anchored about three miles up the river, at a depth equal to the height of the tallest houses in Liverpool. She was not to be seen from Prince's Stage, but I caught a glimpse of her imposing bulk from the first bend in the river.

One would have taken her for a small island, hardly discernible in the mist. She appeared with her bows towards us, having swung round with the tide; but soon the tender altered her course, and the whole length of the steam-ship was presented to our view; she seemed what in fact she was – enormous! Three or four colliers alongside were pouring their cargoes of coal into her port-holes. Beside the *Great Eastern*, these three-mast ships looked like barges; their funnels did not even reach the first line of light-ports in her hull; the yards of their gallant-sails did not come up to her bulwarks. The giant could have hoisted these ships on its davits like shore-boats.

Meanwhile the tender approached the *Great Eastern*, whose chains were violently strained by the pressure of the tide, and ranged up to the foot of an immense winding staircase, on the port side. In this position the deck of the tender was only on a level with the load water-line of the steam-ship, to which line she would be depressed when in full cargo, and which still emerged two yards.

The workmen were now hurriedly disembarking and clambering up the numerous steps which terminated at the fore-part of the ship. I, with head upturned, and my body thrown back, surveyed the wheels of the *Great Eastern*, like a tourist looking up at a high edifice.

Seen from the side, these wheels looked narrow and contracted, although their paddles were four yards broad, but in front they had a monumental aspect. Their elegant fittings, the arrangements of the whole plan, the stays crossing each other to support the division of the triple centre rim, the radius of red spokes, the machinery half lost in the shadow of the wide paddle-boxes, all this impressed the mind, and  awakened an idea of some gigantic and mysterious power.

With what force must these wooden paddles strike the waves which are now gently breaking over them! what a boiling of water when this powerful engine strikes it blow after blow! what a thundering noise engulfed in this paddle-box cavern! when the *Great Eastern* goes at full speed, under the pressure of wheels measuring fifty-three feet in diameter and 166 in circumference, weighing ninety tons, and making eleven revolutions a minute. The tender had disembarked her crew; I stepped on to the fluted iron steps, and in a few minutes had crossed the fore-part of the *Great Eastern*.

Richard Passmore   c1935

Whatever I had learned in my Latin class, in Liverpool all ways led to the Pier Head. I would walk along the stage, feeling the ambient dark and the lights on the oily water: at such times even Mersey water acquired mystery. The ships at anchor would show their riding-lights; from a cabin here and a porthole there a glimmer of light would tell of more-fortunate beings, destined to leave Liverpool far behind and experience remote lands. I, too, wanted to experience remote lands. On the way home I would walk through Lime Street Station, stand at the end of the platform, consider the moonlight outside shining dully on the rails curving away into the unknown world.

Samuel Taylor Coleridge   1812

My dear Friends

How pleasant 'tis to travel brisk! At Stratford upon Avon we were only 9 Hours behind the Mail, having travelled almost but not quite 4 miles an hour. – I breakfasted at Oxford, & stayed more than an hour; but was afraid to send for my nephews, lest they should have been quizzed by their fellow collegiates, such was the Pothouse at which the Stage landed, such the ridiculous appearance of the Coach, with 14 distinct gaudy Pictures painted on it – & we were so followed both in & out of the city by a mob of Boys, shouting out – Lazy Liverpool! Lousy Liverpool–! Here comes long, lazy, lousy Liverpool – ! – And truly the Coach deserves it's honors – Two *such* wretches were forced in on me all night, half drunk, and their Cloathes crusted over with dirt, the best portion of it from the mud into which they had fallen in a squabble, & the worst part filth of their own making. – Two large ticks, i.e. λουσες, I have found on me – & I had taken the precaution to put my bank notes into my breast-plate, but not liking money to lie so near my heart, or to tell the silly truth, not liking it to touch the little remembrancer of affection which I wear there, I therefore put the money into my watch-fob. And sure enough in the night, while dozing, I felt a hand at my small Cloathes – & starting up, the handy Gentleman said, he was

afraid I was cold, & so was only putting up the straw round my Legs. Kind Creature! Meantime, the Guard & Coachman (the last especially) had such ferocious phyzzes, that I thought it prudent not to complain to the Proprietors – so on my arrival here I quitted the Concern, & and have taken a place in the Bang-up for Liverpool at 6 o/clock tomorrow morning. I continued the only inside passenger – & during the day was left pretty much alone – but a precious set would have been crowded in on me during the night. Besides, I itched all over me – & was miserable till I could shift myself, & have my hair combed out by a Hair-dresser.

Graham Greene 1935

The huge Liverpool hotel had been designed without aesthetic taste but with the right ideas about comfort and a genuine idea of magnificence. It could probably house as many passengers as an Atlantic liner; passengers, because no one goes to Liverpool for pleasure, to the little cramped square and the low sky-signs which can almost be touched with the hand, where all the bars and the cinemas close at ten. But there was a character hidden in this hotel; it wasn't chic, it wasn't bright, it wasn't international; there remained somewhere hidden, among its long muffled corridors, beneath the huge cliff-like fall of its walls, the idea of an English inn; one didn't mind asking for muffins or a pint of bitter, while the boats hooted in the Mersey and the luggage littered the hall; there was quite probably a boots. Anyway enough remained for me to understand the surprise of Henry James when he landed in England, 'that England should be as English as, for my entertainment, she took the trouble to be.'

The natural native seediness had not been lost in the glitter of chromium plate; the muffin had been overwhelmingly, perhaps rather nauseatingly, enlarged. If the hotel were silly, it was only because magnificence is almost always a little silly. The magnificent gesture seldom quite comes off. When on rare occasions beauty and magnificence do coincide, one gets a sense of the theatre or the films, it is 'too good to be true'. I find myself always torn between two beliefs: the belief that life should be better than it is and the belief that when it appears better it is really worse. But in the huge lounge at

Liverpool, like the lounge of a country inn fifty times magnified, one was at home on the vast expanse of deep dark carpet, only one business man asleep with his mouth open; at home as one would certainly not have been if the Hollywood imagination had run riot. One was protectively coloured, one was seedy too.

Next morning, in the public-house

near the Prince's Stage, four middle-aged women sat drinking with an old dirty man of eighty-four. Three had the dustbin look; they carried about them the air of tenements, of lean cats and shared wash-houses; the fourth had risen a little way in the world, she was the old man's daughter over from America for Christmas. 'Have another drink, Father?' He was seeing her off. Their relationship was intimate and merry; the whole party had an air of slightly disreputable revelry. To one the party didn't really matter; she had caught the American accent. To the other women, who must return to the dustbin, it was perilous, precarious, breath-taking; they were happy and aghast when the old man drew out a pound note and stood a round himself. 'Well, why shouldn't he?' the daughter asked them, asked Jackie boy, the bar-tender, the beer advertisements, the smutty air, the man who came in selling safety-razor blades, half a dozen for threepence, 'it's better than spending it on a crowd of strange dames.'

The Liverpool waterside at least had not changed since James's day: 'The black steamers knocking about in the yellow Mersey, under a sky so low that they seemed to touch it with their funnels, and in the thickest, windiest light'; – even the colour was the same, 'the grey mildness, shading away into black at every pretext.'

The cargo ship lay right outside the Mersey in the Irish Sea; a cold January wind blew across the tender; people sat crammed together below deck saying good-bye, bored, embarrassed and bonhomous, like parents at a railway station the first day of term, while England slipped away from the port-hole, a stone stage, a tarred side, a slap of grey water against the glass.

William Craft   1860

My wife and myself were both unwell when we left Boston, and, having taken fresh cold on the journey to Halifax, we were laid up there under the doctor's care, nearly the whole fortnight. I had much worry about getting tickets, for they baffled us shamefully at the Cunard office. They at first said that they did not book till the steamer came; which was not the fact. When I called again, they said they knew the steamer would come full from Boston, and therefore we had 'better try to get to Liverpool by other means.' Other mean Yankee excuses were made; and it was not till an influential gentleman, to whom Mr Francis Jackson, of Boston, kindly gave us a letter, went and rebuked them, that we were able to secure our tickets. So when we went on board my wife was very poorly, and was also so ill on the voyage that I did not believe she could live to see Liverpool.

However, I am thankful to say she arrived; and, after laying up at Liverpool very ill for two or three weeks, gradually recovered.

It was not until we stepped upon the shore at Liverpool that we were free from every slavish fear.

William Culshaw Greenhalgh   1853

1853 Wednesday March 9th. I got my luggage on board, had great difficulty in getting it measured, which prevented me procureing a porter in time before the Ship left the Basin, she left me standing along side of my luggage, as if I was to be left. hired a Donkey Cart to take the luggage to Princess Pier, had great trouble with the porters, had engaged them previous was engaged for 1/- and desired 11/-. I was not to be imposed upon and tendered them their 1/- Off I went with the Donkey Cart well loded a distance of 1 mile had not traveled far, when a friend Harry that was with me discovered one of the wheels coming off. he cried out 'whoa' seised

 the wheel I flies to the Donkey's head, fortunately he was not bad to stop, or we should have had an upset, we examined the wheel & found a piece of bone as a substitute for the lin nale of course we had to repair the wheel, had got nothing that whould act, but found by looking about in the street an old can, we twisted the wire that was round the top, & made if fit very well, got Mr. Donkey on his journey once more, my friend watching the wheel I holding the boxes, the Boy coaxing the Donkey, had a great row with the boy, he proved like the rest an imposter, charged 5/- we paid him 1/- & gave him a few coppers to hold his noise, were informed that the tug was not going to the Ship any more, of course in another fix, hired a ferry boat for 10/- Harry & a friend went with the luggage to get it on board arrived along side the Ship, the tide being very high, caused the rope to slip, & was washed down the river a distance of 6 or 7 miles, were expected to be upset the boatman was a complete blaguard, struck them both several times & threatened to pitch them overboard, got the luggage back quiet safe but with great difficulty, charged 10/6 for running the risk of loosing it altogether, the tug left for the Ship at 4 PM, arrived on board all right, met with my Bro Jim

& Mrs was busy arrainging our Births, returned with the tug to Liverpool, spent a pleasant evening together.

*****

Sunday 13th March. The day arrived at last for starting, the tug alongside at 7 AM. weighed Anchor at 7 AM. went ahead at 11 AM government Inspector on board, all passengers ordered on deck, inspected the births, at mustar 1 passenger missing, band commenced playing off she goes the cannons fireing the people on shore cheering shouting hurrah & waving their handkerchiefs others on board in the midst of tears taking the last farewell to England, the Band changed tunes to the Girl I left behind me afterwards Janett & Janoe which caused most of us to look very simple I can assure you.

Samuel Derrick   1760

My Lord,

As I have, no where, met with any accurate account of this very opulent town, perhaps my endeavour to give your lordship something of that sort, may not prove disagreeable.

 Liverpoole stands upon the decline of a hill, about six miles from the sea. It is washed by a broad rapid stream called the Mersee, where ships lying at anchor are quite exposed to the sudden squalls of wind, that often sweep the surface from the flat Cheshire shore on the west, or the high lands of Lancashire that overlook the town on the east; and the banks are so shallow and deceitful, that when once a ship

drives, there is no possibility of preserving her, if the weather prove rough, from being wrecked, even close to the town.

About three years since, a ship outward bound for America, richly laden, being badly piloted, struck and went immediately down. Her mast is still plainly to be seen; but she being effectually sucked in by the sandy bottom, all attempts to weigh her up have been ineffectual.

Frederick Hawkins Piercy 1853

Just as I had completed my survey, there was a general muster for examination by the Government Medical Inspector, the strong and healthy strode up with confidence, answered questions promptly, and in a tone of independence, while the few who had been recently indisposed, nervously advanced, answered warily, and having passed examination, seemed to congratulate themselves, as if they had escaped from some great danger. One very old woman supported by two men was delayed a short time, but as she was only weak from the effects of old age, she was permitted to proceed on her journey of *obedience*. All were healthy, or sufficiently so to warrant them in staying on board. So we were hauled out of dock, and soon after, a pedlar and an old woman with a basket of trinkets were found 'stowed away' on board. The little fat Captain, who turned out to be a choleric old fellow, flew at the man 'like a Turk,' punched his head, and blacked his eye, and sent both man and woman back by steam tug which took us out.

We were quickly towed down the Mersey, past the Rock Lighthouse and the Fort at the mouth, and the wind being fair, the sails were soon unfurled and filled, and we stood out to sea.

Thoughts crowded my brain; of course I thought of old England. It is impossible to leave the land of one's birth without regret, or to leave one's kindred and friends, even for a few months, without a sigh. I wondered whether I should ever see them again, or if my ears would ever again be greeted with gentle words of affection in fond tones from their loving lips!

Henry Dawson 1913

I must have been around five when I was put in the Home. After a few years in this home we were transferred to Olive Mount home. Wavertree, Liverpool. There life started for the four of us, we started school, had a large field to play in, the school had their own band.

Church was held in the big hall in the school, a minister came in from the city to conduct the service – we had a choir and I went in the choir. So I guess that was the first time I knew that I could sing. The home was made up of cottages numbering from A to the end of the alphabet. The four of us were placed in E Cottage – a total of 14 boys to a cottage, we had a lady to look after us, we called her mother. We all had chores to do, as I remember I had the chore to lace up the mother's shoes, and I had to check all the laundry when it came in, put the things that needed mending to one side and I had the job of darning the socks. The older boys polished the shoes for Sunday. The mother had a day off each week – at night the older boys formed a line and started a pillow fight. We certainly got banged around. Then came the time for some of us to be transferred to another home, called the Miss Birds sheltering home. For church service we went to Sun Hall in the city of Liverpool. Then on a Sunday morning as we were having service we were told that it was time for some of us to sail to Canada. I am not sure exactly how many sailed with me. Charlie my twin and brother George came with me. The Home didn't get our first names right. I was named Henry Charles and Charlie was named Charles Henry, as we were twins, but that was all changed when I sent for my birth certificate and the one had my birthday as being in December instead of February. Albert stayed in Liverpool as his health was poor for Colonial life. I don't remember much of the boat trip over, we weren't allowed up on deck but we used to go and visit the cook and get a hot plate of gruel.

Beryl Bainbridge   1983

I stood at the Adelphi window for a long time, looking along the deserted length of Church Street. All the landmarks I remembered, gone without trace. No Boosey and Hawkes with the ukuleles in the window and a life-sized photograph of George Formby, smiling just to show you how easy it was. No gunsmith's with its velvet drapes and pheasants stuffed with sawdust, and Johnny Walker in his breeches, who once had leapt in coloured lights across the hoarding of the public house, toppled forever from the sky. No ice-warehouse, no Bears Paw restaurant, no pet market. Gone the parrot humped in its gilded cage in Blackler's store. Obliterated the gloomy depths of the Kardomah Café; burnt as old-fashioned the red plush sofas of the Lyceum tearooms; slung onto the refuse tips the potted palms and the nickel-plated water jugs.

When the grand scheme of redevelopment was started, the planners had enough cash to pull down the buildings and make the motorways, and they hoped more would be found when the time came to erect houses. But they didn't find it. There isn't the money to buy any more concrete or to maintain what remains. Liverpool isn't the wealthy port it was when my father went as a cabin boy to America. It should have been obvious to a blind moggie, but it wasn't to the planners.

If I were an historian I could chart the reasons for all this chaos: decline of trade, loss of Empire, aeroplanes instead of ships, cars instead of railways, synthetics instead of cotton, the trade unions, the rise of the Japanese. If I were a politician I could blame the Conservatives for greed, the Liberals for lack of confidence, the socialists for naivety and jumping on the bandwagon of progress. But it hardly matters now. It's too late. Someone's murdered Liverpool and got away with it.

Joseph Ballard 1815

I took my passage on Saturday in the coach for Warrington eighteen miles distant from Liverpool. The gardens and fields looked delightful being in quite as forward a state of vegetation as ours in June. I was much amused at the activity of the tumbling boys who turned head over heels at the side of the coach and with such swiftness as to even keep up with it for some time, which is done in expectation that the passengers will throw them a penny, their parents beings so miserably poor that this is resorted to as a means of subsistence.

Alan Bennett   1985

28 July. It is nine o'clock and still light, and I go looking for
a restaurant to have my supper. I walk through the terrible
St John's Centre. It has a restaurant, set on a concrete pole
(may the architect rot); now empty, it boasts a tattered notice
three hundred feet up advertising to passing seagulls that it
is TO LET. I pass three children, the eldest about twelve. They
are working on a shop window which has CLOSING
DOWN painted on it. Spelling obviously not their strong
point, they are standing back from it puzzling how they can
turn it into an obscenity when I pass with my book. The book
takes their eye and there's a bit of 'Look at him. He's got a
book.' 'What's your book?' I walk on and find myself in an
empty precinct. The children have stopped taunting and
seem to have disappeared. I look round and find that the trio
are silently keeping pace with me. In an utterly empty square
they are no more than three
feet away. I am suddenly
alarmed, stop, and turn back
to where there are more
people. I have never done
that before in England, and
not even in New York.

John Wray   1818

When we got to the house we were introduced into a drinking room with good seats around it. There were not any
people there except ourselves and two men, who had come
with us on the packet. My wife proceeded to put the children

to bed first thing as they were sleepy. After that we had a little spirit and water and proceeded to bed. We had a double bedded room to ourselves and three of the children slept along with other people. I had a tolerable night and the children, but my wife rested but middling, and in the morning to her great trouble and mortification, she was much bitten with bugs, so that her face was disfigured and one eye nearly swelled up, and very uncomfortable she felt with it, after lying in these uncomfortable beds from twelve o'clock to about half after seven, the 20th. In the morning I got up and cleaned the childrens' shoes and when they were dressed and came down stairs, we were introduced into a front room to ourselves; but it was a dark close place, but we were more comfortable than in the other rooms that we had been in.

Derek Jewell   1973

They're closing the Cavern in Liverpool, where The Beatles grew and the condensation ran down the stone walls in rivulets. And I was remembering, oh, round about 1961,

when little Paul McCartney was singing and looking as though butter wouldn't melt in his mouth, and the girl beside me gave the Cavern the beady eye and said: 'They tell me this place used to be a fruit warehouse, and no expense has been spared to leave it just like it was.'

James Bisset 1907

Liverpool, Hamburg, and Bremen were the main exit-ports of the emigrants from northern and central continental Europe and the British Isles. The Cunard Line had also several passenger-vessels transporting migrants westwards across the Atlantic from the Mediterranean ports of southern Europe.

Our third-class passengers were picturesque in their variety of garb and racial features, as they plodded up the gangway in seemingly endless procession, carrying bundles of luggage which perhaps contained all their possessions. Their accommodation down below, though certainly not luxurious, was fair enough at the price, with meals included. A week's discomfort was endurable for the benefit presently to be attained, of becoming Americans. Some would be millionaires there, and some hoboes, but the magic word 'America' lured them all, and adventure was in their hearts.

Anthony Burgess 1943

The view of Liverpudlians that they are a race apart is well-founded. There is the unanalysable genetic mixture of a great port and also Welsh from the south and Irish a jump across from Dublin. The speech is distinctive. 'All got your furs, love?' cried the tram conductresses, who kept warm with a bit of moth-eaten fare. The energy is immense and explains the gratuitous violence. The fighting O'Sullivans were introduced to me as a family that had a fight before they went to bed. One of them were a lad who liked to fight with 'is 'ead, but once he got it torn with his opponent's fish 'ooks. Terrible, terrible. Generosity could lead to violence. If I asked a direction I would soon have a crowd around me giving contradictory instructions. I would leave a fight behind and have to ask again.

Thomas Cather 1836

February 1836 – Owing to hard gales blowing from the westward, we were detained several days in Liverpool, greatly to our discomfort, not merely because Liverpool is a very dull place, but on account of the unpleasant state of uncertainty in which we were placed, not knowing at what hour we might start. But on Thursday, the 4th of February 1836, the wind having shifted to the N.E., we were enabled to leave the dock, but had scarcely got our sails set, and were not more than

two miles from port, when a Maltese ran foul of us and carried away some of our rigging. In consequence of this misfortune we were obliged to put back to have the damage repaired. If one tithe of the curses that were launched against the Maltese had taken effect he must have gone to the bottom, for deep and bitter were the maledictions which issued from our captain and crew. Henry and I had been so much annoyed by having been obliged to go every day to the docks to ascertain when the ship would sail that we determined on remaining on board.

As people should always accommodate themselves to circumstances, and as the best philosophy in this world is to make oneself as comfortable as possible wherever one is, we determined to act on that plan, and to commence it that very day. The other passengers, having friends in Liverpool, went on shore to enjoy their society for another night; but we had few friends on English ground, our luggage was on board the good ship *North America*, commanded by the tight seaman Captain Dixey, and there our interest was, so we determined on remaining on board and making ourselves as comfortable as possible. After having discussed the merits of a brace of fowls and seen the bottom of a flask of champagne, we fell into a pleasant and most edifying discourse on a great variety of topics, of which speculations touching our future rambles constituted a principal share. A bottle of brandy, some hot water and sugar, flanked by a copious dessert of choice fruit, were laid on the table. The water in the jug was *fizzing hot*, the fire in the stove was burning bright, the brandy in the decanter was sparkling most invitingly, and the lumps of white sugar seemed almost melting with desire to become more intimately acquainted with the brandy. So we did as all men with any regard to their own comfort would do. We pulled off our boots, cased our feet in fur-lined slippers (for the night was very cold), drew our chairs close round the stove, mixed each a glass of punch, and (having satisfied ourselves of the proper strength and flavour) placed our feet on the fender and whiled away the time by laying plans for the future – an occupation that is so often fruitless.

We retired to bed at a reasonable hour, but were disturbed about midnight by a most extraordinary noise, which commenced with a low humming note, then brisked up to something like a concert of penny trumpets, and at last burst forth into a wild howling dirge most terrible to hear. There was on board a quadroon woman, from the Island of Barbadoes, in the capacity of stewardess' assistant, named Tabitha Tapeworm, who had a most inordinate affection for the brandy bottle. After we had retired to our cabin she had got hold of the liquor which her soul loved, and under its potent influence 'kicked up the bobbery' which so much startled us. In fact she fairly played the devil, and broke things. However, she made the amends honourable next morning, apologised for the disturbance she had occasioned, and assured us on her honour that it should not happen again. Next morning we set sail.

Samuel Curwen   1780

The whole complexion nautical and so infinitely below all our expectations that naught but the thoughts of the few hours we had to pass here rendered it tolerable. The Docks, however, are stupendously grand. The inner, or that called Town dock lying amost in the center of it, and is filled with innumerable vessells exhibiting a forrest of masts. Beside this are 3 or 4 very large ones, all containing great numbers of vessells, lying in front of city, communicating with each other by flood gates, inter-mixed with dry ones for benefit of repairing. The lower or new one, of greatest extent has a fine wide Quay on its outer seabord side, an agreeable walk, lined with trees on either hand. Below this in river is now building, almost finisht, a circular battery with embrasures for more than 30 Canon of 32, 24 and 18 pounders. Parade and barracks are now in hand and when compleated, will provide a charming walk and prospect to inhabitants if allowed.

Taking a circuits ramble through this, to us disgustful, at

least to me, plan, returned to Inn paid bill and entered carriage we came in which, Master Driver and owner would fain but for Judge and S.S. resolution have jockeyed us out of (N.B. the people in this Island are perfect masters in their respective line of business) designing craftily to shift us to the common stage but his plan being disappointed we were replaced in our own carriage, with no Company but ourselves.

Bidding a cheerful adieu to Liverpool set forward and in nearly the same that we measured the distance from Prescot returned thither and taking a relay here proceeded to Warrington, innd at our Drivers house, he being owner of stage and innkeeper too.

Alexis de Tocqueville   1835

Liverpool. Town destined to become the centre of English trade. A fisherman's harbour three centuries ago. A small town sixty years ago. The slave trade, basis of its commerical greatness. It carried slaves to the Spanish colonies at better prices than all the others. The foundation of the United States, the manufacturing develop- ment of Manchester and Birmingham, and the spread of English trade over the whole world, have done the rest.

Liverpool is a beautiful town. Poverty is almost as great as it is at Manchester, but it is hidden. Fifty thousand poor people live in cellars. Sixty thousand Irish Catholics.

Edward Elgar   1924

Dear Sir

I am much honoured by the invitation of your committee; I cannot accept the post of President. Alfred Rodewald was a very dear friend and if it were possible to carry on, under his name, some Orchestral Concerts I should be proud to be associated with the executive. Chamber music, in this case, is inadequate and it is a reproach to the musical taste of Liverpool that the Orchestral Concerts should have been allowed to disappear.

Johann Georg Kohl   1844

I cannot tell how many flags were hoisted on the following morning at the different piers of Liverpool, to inform the several passengers where to look for the Glasgow boat, the Isle of Man boat, the Dublin boat, the Cork boat, the Pembroke boat, and all the rest of them. I for my part ranged myself under the flag of Bangor, the most frequented place of transit, to those about to visit North Wales. Uninvited assistants, among whom no doubt were some of the thieves of whom I spoke a few pages back, together with beggars, and other importunate solicitors, surrounded us, and took care that our roses on that morning should not be without thorns. Newsmen offered us the news of the same morning. Others had telescopes for those who wished to contemplate the Welsh coast at their ease. Oranges and gingerbread, with other delicacies of the same kind, were hawked about, and altogether the noise and apparent confusion were enough to make a man run away in despair. The steamers, meanwhile, were humming, hissing, and shrieking around us, but with all their noise and well known vigour, they lay not the less quiet and orderly at their several places, and gradually as the ear and eye became familiarised with it, the noisy bustling scene became a source of amusement and pleasurable excitement.

Yvonne Foley

c1946

My mum married the man I have always thought of as my dad when I was two. My mum, my dad, my sister and I all lived in one room in Liverpool 8. I can remember being ill a lot when I was young. Perhaps that was due to the conditions we lived in then. Not too much different from the conditions many people in the city had to live in at that time.

I found out years later that lots of us Eurasian kids (the children of Chinese fathers and western mothers) lived in the area. Most of their fathers, like mine, had been forced to leave Liverpool. But I didn't know that at the time. I know now that many of our mothers were destitute and not all the kids had parents as good as mine. Some of the women had to work at two and more jobs to keep their families.

The kids in that street were a real mixed bunch – West

Indians, Chinese and Eurasians like me. At the time, of course, I didn't know I was a Eurasian. I thought that one of the boys I used to play with was Chinese. But he wasn't. He was a Eurasian like me – and I met him again after 50 years. That was just a couple of years ago. We call each other every week now.

Over the last few years I have been lucky enough to meet up with some of those who, like me, are the children of Chinese seamen who tried to settle in Liverpool. I think we all feel that meeting each other has given us another family. It is difficult to explain what it is like. Even though we are all different we have something in common that nobody else can share. It is not just that we all grew up in what now would be regarded as terrible poverty. It is to do with what we are and what that meant to us as we grew up. It is something that you cannot explain to others who did not share that experience.

We all agreed that we wanted to have a record of what happened to our mothers and our genetic fathers. Forcing the men out was not something to be proud of. I know it was a product of the time – the racial and class prejudices of the 1940s. But it marked our lives and those of our mothers and fathers.

Benjamin Silliman   1805

I found some amusement yesterday in witnessing the embarkation of a regiment of cavalry. The horses were hoisted in by means of a canvas bag which was made to surround the body of the animal, and tied with ropes over the back. To these ropes a tackle was fastened, and the horses were thus raised from the ground. When they first felt the lifting, they flounced and kicked violently, but, the instant their feet were cleared of the ground, they became perfectly still as if dead, and hung dangling in the air, till they were gently lowered into the hold next the keel.

Steven Gerrard   1989

Every time I drive into Anfield, I slow to a crawl as I pass through the Shankly Gates. My eyes are drawn towards the Hillsborough Memorial. I see the tributes to the ninety-six Liverpool fans who never returned from that FA Cup semi-final in 1989. I see the scarves left by visiting fans, signs of respect that lie alongside wreaths placed by families whose tears will never dry. I see the flame that burns always, reminding the world that the ninety-six will never, ever be forgotten.

As my car inches past the Memorial, I look down the names of those who fell on the Leppings Lane End, never to rise again. My eyes stop at one name. Jon-Paul Gilhooley, ten years old, the youngest of those who never came home from Sheffield. A fan who died following the team he loved. A boy whose life was snatched away just as it was starting. Crushed to death in a stand unfit for human beings. I knew

Jon-Paul. He was my cousin. A shiver runs down my spine. I make the sign of the Cross and drive on.

William Ewart Gladstone c1815

I have seen wild roses growing upon the very ground that is now the centre of the borough of Bootle. All that land is now partly covered with residences and partly with places of business and industry; but in my time but one single house stood upon the space between Primrose brook and the town of Liverpool.

Mark Twain 1879

We arrived in Liverpool an hour ago very tired, and have halted at this hotel (by the advice of misguided friends) – and if my instinct and experience are worth anything, it is the very worst hotel on earth, without any exception. We shall move to another hotel early in the morning to spend to-morrow. We sail for America next day in the *Gallia*.

Hugh Walpole 1907

I went out and down to the Mersey, and there, looking at the river, I had one of the most important hours of my life. That foaming flood tossing in grey froth and spume out to the sea was invincibly strong and mighty. Ships of all sizes were passing; gulls were wheeling with hoarse screams above my head – the sun broke the clouds and suddenly the river was violet with silver lines and circles.

At that moment I knew. The ferry arrived from the other side; people pushed out and past me. The life and bustle and beauty of the world was everywhere about me. I loved it; I adored it; but not for me to try and change it.

Looking out to sea where a great liner slowly took the sun like a queen, I vowed that I would be a novelist, good or bad, for the remainder of my earthly days.

Henry Green   c1928

They had come on tram to outskirts of Liverpool. They were walking in the direction back in now. They looked for address of shop. Mr Jones knew his way. Smell of the sea was at her, forcing itself on her.

They had been on edge of the Residential District. They were coming now to blinded shops. Roads were broader, lighter by a little. Here was dropsical fatness of shopkeepers' paunches, when they got to address they were looking for they knocked one up. Early to bed early to rise this one's motto. In nightshirt he came to window above. He leaned paunch out over window frame, he let his weight sink on it, bulging. If they'd wait two minutes he would get address for them where their parents had moved and in his place at window showed curling papers like bobbins. Whining voice came from inside of that room – 'what is it ma? Ma, ma, who's there ma, what is it?' His wife poked her nose over window frame. Lily saw nose, one eye, curling papers.

'Well now' said fat shopkeeper they met afterwards squirming along in shadows of the street looking for a bit of fun – these courting couples in the doorways y'know, y'know you can see a bit o' fun o' nights – 'well now' he said, 'it's Mulgrave Street you want is it?' He told them, shopkeeper they had knocked up hadn't been able to tell them way to address he had given them and Mr Jones did not know that part of town it was in. Dropsically fat, hatpin little eyes, shopkeeper watched Miss Gates as he told them. Something up here. That gal looked frightened out of her life. But that young chap was up to a bit o' fun. Didn't know how to start with 'er, that's 'ow it looked. Yum yum he felt in huge belly, um yum.

Now first that feeling which had soaked all through about Mr Jones, how everything, everything was wonderful, she was the sweetest girl in the world and wouldn't the old people be glad to see her, now first that feeling ebbed and died in him. He was afraid for her as now they were going into poorer quarter of the town, streets were getting now to be the streets of ports, darkness of waters looked now to be flowing over into these streets. He did not know the way, but he knew they were going towards the docks. He had seen in his mind their coming to that shop and those there telling him to go back the way he had come with Miss Gates, to go back in direction of the Residential District. In his heart picture had warmed him of his bringing Lily to quiet respectable shop in a quiet decent street. He had thought out two ways of turning off her surprise and admiration when she saw so much prosperity. 'It's simple,' was one thing he was going to say, 'it's simple but the old folks knows what's comfortable.' One thing he had always feared, and that was effect his father would have on Miss Gates and now, as they walked further, and the streets were poorer and poorer streets, it was his father he suspected as having thrown his ma's prosperity away.

Ship's syren sounded, wailing, and with a great pang Miss Gates thought a factory buzzer at this time of the night, it couldn't be nightshift at this time of the night, O she did feel afraid. And that man they had asked their way of, his eyes! How dark it was gettting! Well she just wouldn't look any more if it only made her shivery, she just woudn't notice anything more. But it didn't happen often, did it, that all you thought of worst came to pass. But then she thought it wasn't quite so bad, they'd not expected to find them first go off. All the same, these streets! Well, she wouldn't look that's all.

James Hanley   c1930

Mr Anderson had not visited the company's offices which were situated on the Pier-Head, for over five years. The offices were sandwiched in between those of Hastie & Co., General Carriers, and Hunger & Want, the big shipbuilding and repairing firm. Consequently, when on this rainy morning he caught the tram and jumped off at the corner of Water Street, he was somewhat astonished not only to find the original building grown in size but that others of like stature were ranged alongside it, the building with the dome standing out especially as a kind of architectural accident rather than design, a form of hugeness and greatness that concealed rottenness, harboured energy, and measured its greatness by each exacting sweat-drop. Mr Anderson was bewildered. It was just after nine o'clock. A continual stream of black-coated clerks and gaily dressed typists were hurrying towards this giant of a building, wherein they disappeared, not to appear again until evening. It was like a tremendous mouth, ever open, that day after day absorbed so many thousand fragments of human consciousness, and drained them, and dried them up.

Mr Anderson walked slowly down Water Street and crossed the road. The middle of this road was now lined with cars, belonging to officials, major and minor, of the company. Ahead of him he saw the huge swing-doors for the first time. He approached warily, as though he were a felon bent on some dark deed. When he reached the steps – there were twenty of them – he stopped and looked up. The terrific size of the building at once made his own relationship with the universe painfully obvious. He was a mere pigmy, a unit, a fragmentary part of this huge body. He felt outside, lonely, terribly lonely. He wondered if there was anybody in the office whom he might know. He had had at one time, and the offices were much smaller then, the daily job of walking down from the dock to the office with the daily returns of work aboard whatever ship happened to be working by. He knew one or two people who might still be in the same position in the office. He secretly hoped they were still with the company. They could not fail to recognise him. With this thought dominant in his mind, and the precious piece of paper clutched tightly in his trembling hand, he slowly mounted the steps.

Charles Dickens   1842

I wish, Mac – I wish, and I must say it, though you be never so gloomy when you get this – that you could conceive, and from personal inspection were in a condition to understand, the wild absurdity of our 'cabin'. I don't know what to compare it with. A small box at a coffee room is much too big. So is a hackney coach. So is a chariot cab. It is more like one of those cabs where you get in at the back; but I think

you could put on a shirt in one of those: and you certainly couldn't in this chamber. There are two horse-hair seats in it, fixed to the wall – one opposite the other. Either would serve for a kettle holder. The beds (one above the other of course) might both be sent to you per post, with one additional stamp. The pillows are no thicker than crumpets; and the sheets and blankets are too ridiculous to write of.

Our luggage is all aboard. They were 'taking in the Milk' when we [were] there – an enormous cow! Bread, boxes, greens, and bullocks-heads for soup, were strewn about the deck. The grand impression was the smallness of the vessel. The Saloon is nothing like that of a Ramsgate boat – there!!

Elizabeth Pasto Hummer 1912

The year was 1912. The White Star Line was scheduled to launch a fabulous new ship on its maiden voyage to America. The ship was named *Titanic* and for months had been extolled as the largest, most luxurious, fastest, and safest ship ever built. Tickets were soon sold out for the 2500 passenger list, with many very wealthy and notable passengers booked for first class. Unable to get passage on this splendid new ship, the family had to settle for a lesser ship sailing three weeks earlier with a stop in Liverpool, England, the headquarters city of the White Star Line. It was there that Tarmo, age 5, wandered off, causing great pandemonium as the family searched frantically before finding him blithely exploring the sights and sounds of a large industrial city. With no further mishaps, our ship arrived in the New York harbor well before my birth date of May 12th.

Washington Irving 1815

No sooner did I hear of the interesting group that had come out in the *Minerva Smyth*, than, with my usual excitement, which is apt to put me in a fever, and make me overshoot my mark, I got a boat and set off for the ship, which lay about three miles off. The weather was boisterous – the Mersey rough. I got well ducked; and, when I arrived on board, had the satisfaction to hear that my eagerness had, as usual, led me upon a wild-goose chase, and that, had I made the least inquiry, I should have found the passengers had all landed early in the morning. Away then I paddled across the river; and the tide being contrary, was landed at the upper part of

Liverpool; had to trudge two miles through dirty lanes and alleys; was two or three times entangled among the docks, and baulked by draw-bridges thrown open, so that it was afternoon before I got to the Liverpool Arms, where I found the party all comfortably housed.

Henry James   1899

There were people on the ship with whom he had easily consorted– so far as ease could up to now be imputed to him – and who for the most part plunged straight into the current that set from the landing-stage to London; there were others who had invited him to a tryst at the inn and had even invoked his aid for a 'look round' at the beauties of Liverpool; but he had stolen away from every one alike, had kept no appointment and renewed no acquaintance, had been indifferently aware of the number of persons who esteemed themselves fortunate in being, unlike himself, 'met', and had even independently, unsociably, alone, without encounter or relapse and by mere quiet evasion, given his afternoon and evening to the immediate and sensible. They formed a qualified draught of Europe, an afternoon and an evening on the banks of the Mersey, but such as it was he took his potion at least undiluted.

Fanny Kemble   1830

You probably have by this time heard and read accounts of the opening of the railroad, and the fearful accident which occurred at it, for the papers are full of nothing else. The accident you mention *did* occur, but though the unfortunate man who was killed bore Mr. Stephenson's name, he was not related to him. I will tell you something of the events on the 15th, as, though you may be acquainted with the circumstances of poor Mr. Huskisson's death, none but an eye-witness of the whole scene can form a conception of it. I told you that we had had places given to us, and it was the main purpose of our returning from Birmingham to Manchester to be present at what promised to be one of the most striking events in the scientific annals of our country. We started on Wednesday last, to the number of about eight hundred people, in carriages constructed as I before described to you. The most intense curiosity and excitement prevailed, and, though the weather was uncertain, enormous masses of densely packed people lined the road, shouting and waving hats and handkerchiefs as we flew by them. What with the sight and sound of these cheering multitudes and the tremendous velocity with which we were borne past them, my spirits rose to the true champagne height, and I never enjoyed anything so much as the first hour of our progress. I had been unluckily separated from my mother in the first distribution of places, but by an exchange of seats which she was enabled to make she rejoined me when I was at the height of my ecstasy, which was considerably damped by finding that she was frightened to death, and intent upon nothing but devising means of escaping from a situation which appeared to her to threaten with instant annihilation herself and all her travelling companions. While I was chewing the cud of this disappointment, which was rather bitter, as I had expected her to be as delighted as myself with our excursion, a man flew by us, calling out through a speak-

ing-trumpet to stop the engine, for that somebody in the directors' carriage had sustained an injury. We were all stopped accordingly, and presently a hundred voices were heard exclaiming that Mr. Huskisson was killed; the confusion that ensued is indescribable: the calling out from carriage to carriage to ascertain the truth, the contrary reports which were sent back to us, the hundred questions eagerly uttered at once, and the repeated and urgent demands for surgical assistance, created a sudden turmoil that was quite sickening. At last we distinctly ascertained that the unfortunate man's thigh was broken. From Lady W—, who was in the duke's carriage, and within three yards of the spot where the accident happened, I had the following details, the horror of witnessing which we were spared through our situation behind the great carriage. The engine had stopped to take in a supply of water, and several of the gentlemen in the directors' carriage had jumped out to look about them. Lord W—, Count Batthyany, Count Matuscenitz, and Mr. Huskisson among the rest were standing talking in the middle of the road, when an engine on the other line, which was parading up and down merely to show its speed, was seen coming down upon them like lightning. The most active of those in peril sprang back into their seats: Lord W— saved his life only by rushing behind the duke's carriage, and Count Matuscenitz had but just leaped into it, with the engine all but touching his heels as he did so; while poor Mr. Huskisson, less active from the effects of age and ill health, bewildered, too, by the frantic cries of 'Stop the engine! Clear the track!' that resounded on all sides, completely lost his head, looked helplessly to the right and left, and was instantaneously prostrated by the fatal machine, which dashed down like a thunderbolt upon him, and passed over his leg, smashing and mangling it in the most horrible way. (Lady W— said she distinctly heard the crushing of the bone.) So terrible was the effect of the appalling accident that, except that ghastly 'crushing' and poor Mrs. Huskisson's piercing shriek, not a sound was heard or a word uttered among the immediate spectators of the catastrophe. Lord W— was the first to raise the poor sufferer, and calling to aid his surgical skill, which is considerable, he tied up the severed artery, and for a time, at least, prevented death by loss of blood. Mr. Huskisson was then placed in a carriage with his wife and Lord W—, and the engine, having been detached from the director's carriage, conveyed them to Manchester.

Carolyn Irvine   1953

I have a small black and white photograph taken from the overhead railway which shows the *Empress of Canada* lying on its side in Gladstone dock. In 1953, this liner caught fire during an overhaul in the dock, and the amount of water used in extinguishing the fires caused it to heel over.

My father, Bill Colbeck, was hydrographical surveyor for the Mersey Docks and Harbour Board, and with his team of engineers, devised a unique system for righting and refloating this large ship. The week before the raising we all had to be very quiet in the house – no shouting or squabbling because it was such a tense time for my father. All eyes were on him, and on 6th March 1954, the *Empress of Canada* was finally towed out of the dock and into the Mersey.

During the Second World War, my father's job was classed

 as a reserved occupation, too important for him to rejoin the Navy. Liverpool would become the most important convoy base for the North Atlantic, and keeping the shipping lanes open and operating in the face of enemy attack required the most experienced surveyors and salvage experts to remain on shore dealing with the daily problems caused by enemy action.

The river was an intrinsic part of family life, too. On Christmas Day, whilst my mother prepared our Christmas lunch, my father would take us children with him as he visited the salvage ships and depots where his men were on duty. Each man was presented with a Christmas cigar. We usually got a drink of orange squash and a biscuit! And at midnight on New Year's Eve we were taken outside so we could hear the ships' hooters welcoming the New Year.

In 1948 my father became Marine Surveyor and Water

Bailiff for the Board. In this capacity he oversaw the continuing mapping of Liverpool Bay and the Mersey Estuary, and he was responsible for the introduction of the Port Radar system for Liverpool and the rest of the Mersey. He was known as 'Mr Mersey' – the man who kept the Mersey open during the war.

Sinclair Lewis   1910

The SS *Merian* panted softly beside the landing-stage at Birkenhead, resting in the sunshine after her voyage, while the cattle were unloaded. They had encountered fog-banks at the mouth of the Mersey River. Mr Wrenn had ecstatically watched the shores of England – *England!* – ride at him through the fog, and had panted over the lines of English villas among the dunes. It was like a dream, yet the shore had such amazingly safe solid colours, real red and green and yellow, when contrasted with the fog-wet deck unearthily glancing with mist-lights.

Now he was seeing his first foreign city, and to Morton, stolidly curious beside him, he could say nothing save 'Gee!' With church-tower and swarthy dome behind dome, Liverpool lay across the Mersey. Up through the Liverpool streets that ran down to the river, as though through peep-holes slashed straight back into the Middle Ages, his vision plunged, and it wandered unchecked through each street while he hummed: 'Free, free, in Eu-ro-pee, that's *me*!'

The cattlemen were called to help unload the remaining hay. They made a game of it. Even Satan smiled, even the Jewish elders were lightly affable as they made pretendedly fierce gestures at the squat patient hay-bales. Tim, the hatter, danced a limber foolish jig upon the deck, and McGarver bellowed, 'The bon-nee, bon-nee banks of Loch Lo-o-o-mond.'

The crowd bawled: 'Come on, Bill Wrenn; your turn. Hustle up with that bale, Pete, or we'll sic Bill on you.'

Bill Wrenn, standing very dignified, piped: 'I'm Colonel Armour. I own all these cattle, 'cept the Morris uns, see? Gotta do what I say, savvy? Tim, walk on your ear.'

The hatter laid his head on the deck and waved his anaemic legs in accordance with directions from Colonel Armour (late Wrenn).

The hay was off. The *Merian* tooted and headed across the Mersey to the Huskinson Dock, in Liverpool, while the cattlemen played touch about the deck. Whooping and laughing, they made last splashy toilets at the water-butts, dragged out their luggage, and descended to the dock-house.

As the cattlemen passed Bill Wrenn and Morton, shouting affectionate good-byes in English or courteous Yiddish, Bill commented profanely to Morton on the fact that the solid stone floor of the great shed seemed to have enough sea-motion to 'make a guy sick.' It was nearly his last utterance as Bill Wrenn. He became Mr Wrenn, absolute Mr Wrenn, on the street, as he saw a real English bobby, a real English carter, and the sign, 'Cocoa Rooms. Tea 1*d*.'

England!

'Now for some real grub!' cried Morton. 'No more scouse and willow-leaf tea.'

Stretching out their legs under a table glorified with toasted Sally Lunns and Melton Mowbrays, served by a waitress who said 'Thank *you*' with a rising inflexion, they gazed at the line of mirrors running Britishly all around the room over the long lounge seat, and smiled with the triumphant content which comes to him whose hunger for dreams and hunger for meat-pies are satisfied together.

Malcolm Lowry   c1928

As he passes down Church Street the wind rushes round him with a cold, monstrous, final insistency. He walks without thinking where he is going. Tramlines run in front of the offices; mothers with warm-smelling furs are fussing with their school-capped sons into the Bon Marché; further away secret tunnels bore through the gloomy buildings, and the overhead railway and a number of sloping bridges leading to the landing stage spread round in bleak and bare confusion. Tram bells clang. Brutal buildings stride into the air above Dana Hilliot.... But the wind has enveloped and overarched all these masses of iron and concrete, all this little humanity, and is sweeping these sparkling buildings with rushing, tremendous shadows. '*Yacko*,' shout the newsboys, wearing, like aprons, the announcement: 'Norwegian liner aground in Mersey!' 'Last *Echo Exprey*!' He retreats up Church Street, Castle Street, down old Ropery again. The wind blows up from the road an old copy of the *Liverpool Express*, rumples and whisks it down the Goree Piazzas. It clings finally to a lamppost, like some ugly, cringing wraith. The lamppost was an erect viper, poised in climax of anger, to bite.... Crowds drift to and from the ferries, battling with the wind, their coats whipping round their knees, or blowing over their heads. A drove of black cattle clatter past, herded by a hooligan with a twisted stick. A dockside train with its diminutive engine is rumbling along cautiously beneath the Overhead Railway bridges in the direction of Mann Island and the Canning Dock, the sinister bell of warning singing out its desolate nostalgic phrase, *y'lang y'lang y'lang y'lang*.

Anne Tuttle Jones Bullard 1850

The captain told us that on his last trip from Liverpool to New

York, among seven hundred passengers, he found that seven had been smuggled on board, but it was discovered too late to set them adrift. Sometimes a man is headed up in a barrel – he has known a man to be put in a sack and filled around with potatoes, and sometimes done up in feather beds and other luggage. Whenever he sees any suspicious looking bundles on board, he sends a man with a long stick that has two or three prongs to it, to stick into the luggage, and ascertain if it contains a piece of humanity.

Jonathan Meades 2007

After the garden festival came the renovation of its dock

buildings – which are of a grandeur unmatched in Britain. The endurance of these awesome structures serves only to make trade and empire seem all the more fragile, all the more fugitive. They are visible reminders of what once was and now isn't: a city's greatness. They end up, however, as monuments to industrial impotence against which the bereft present is forced to measure itself.

John Newton   1754

I had the pleasure to return thanks in the churches (at Liverpool), for an African voyage, performed without any accident, or the loss of a single man; and it was much noticed and acknowledged in the town. I question if it is not the only instance of the kind. When I made my first appearance upon 'Change, a stranger would have thought me a person of great importance, by the various congratulations I received from almost every gentleman present.

My stay at home was intended to be but short, and by the beginning of November I was ready again for the sea; but the Lord saw fit to overrule my design. During the time I was engaged in the slave trade, I never had the least scruple as to its lawfulness. I was, upon the whole, satisfied with it, as the appointment Providence had marked out for me; yet it was in many respects far from eligible. It is, indeed, accounted a genteel employment, and is usually very profitable, though to me it did not prove so, the Lord seeing that a large increase of wealth could not be good for me. However, I considered myself as a sort of gaoler or turnkey; and I was sometimes shocked with an employment that was perpetually conversant with chains, bolts, and shackles. In this view, I had often petitioned, in my prayers, that the Lord (in his own time) would be pleased to fix me in a more humane calling, and (if it might be) place me where I might have more frequent converse with his people and ordinances, and be freed from those long separations from home, which very often were hard to bear.

Nathaniel Hawthorne 1853

The Mersey has the color of a mud-puddle, and no atmospheric effect, as far as I have seen, ever gives it a more agreeable tinge.

John Owen c1912

Presently they were rolling on beside the overhead electric railway, which links the southernmost with northernmost docks. The roar of the trains, like that of a torrent above their heads, could be heard almost continuously, while often they caught a flash from the power rail. Presently their progress became slower, and at times they were held up altogether to allow of the passage of some great tandem horse lorry on which, built up like blocks of granite in the walls of a house, rose bales of the cotton – each four foot square and bound in tattered wrapping of hemp – with which Weftport sought interminably to satisfy the raging hunger of Lancashire. In Mary's present mood, in her new awareness of the underlying romance and adventure of this life of trade, the sight of the first of these great loads of American cotton, bale piled above bale, gave her an extraordinary thrill. It was significant of so much this morning – even of everything – of this man she had married and of the child propped here beside her and looking on so calmly and unknowingly.

She was what she was because of these crude pluckings from plants in far away places over there in the 'West.' Not merely the fine linens with which she covered herself, and her son, and with which she decorated her house, owed their existence in this their perfected state to such bales as rolled heavily by; but she – creature of fair flesh that she was – owed also.

Edward Patey 1964

It is not usual to receive letters of condolence on accepting an appointment which would generally be seen as a promotion. Yet that is what happened when some of my friends read in the press that I was going to be Dean of Liverpool. They wondered why I should want to leave Coventry, with all the excitement and world-wide interest surrounding the new cathedral, to go to Liverpool where the huge unfinished sandstone edifice was already in danger of becoming a dinosaur surviving from another age, an Edwardian *folie de grandeur* out of tune with the mood of the second half of the twentieth century.

Louisa May Alcott   c1865

We only stopped at Liverpool a few hours. It's a dirty, noisy place, and I was glad to leave it. Uncle rushed out and bought a pair of dog-skin gloves, some *ugly*, thick shoes, and an umbrella, and got shaved *à la* mutton chop, the first thing. Then he flattered himself that he looked like a true Briton; but the first time he had the mud cleaned off his shoes, the little boot-black knew that an American stood in them, and said, with a grin, 'There yer har, sir. I've given 'em the latest Yankee shine.' It amused uncle immensely.

Reverend Thomas Raffles   1840

On the 19th of February, 1840, the first Great George Street Chapel was utterly destroyed by fire. How the fire originated was, I believe, never satisfactorily ascertained, though the probability is that it arose from the apparatus which was introduced for warming the chapel. Unhappily, it was not insured for more than £4,000, and even that would have been lost, had it not been for the somewhat remarkable circumstances which I am now about to relate. On the Friday evening before the fire, there was a meeting of the Juvenile Missionary Society held in the schoolroom under the chapel, at which I presided. At that meeting I observed a young man – evidently, from his dress, a working man – sitting, throughout the whole of the evening, apart. Occupied with the business of the meeting, I thought but little of this circumstance, though it arrested my attention; but when the meeting was over, I observed that he still remained, occupying the same position as he had kept throughout. This induced me to inquire what was his business there, when I was told that he was the person sent to look after the stoves which had been recently introduced into the building. That answer at once brought to my mind the subject of the insurance. 'By-the-by,' I said to Mr Samuel Job, 'have those stoves ever been reported at the insurance offices?' On his replying in the negative, I requested that the necessary steps might be taken immediately to make all sure. Notice was given at the offices on the following day (Saturday). The next day, being Sunday, of course nothing was done. Monday passed without any action on their part, but on Tuesday the agents came, surveyed and reported; an indorsement was made on the policies, accepting the premises as they then were, and on the next morning, Wednesday, they were totally consumed. One of the agents, Mr Wallace Currie, actually sent up to London notice of the acceptance of the insurance, and of the destruction of the chapel by the same post. 'Pretty fellows you are,' he said to me, 'to insure your chapel one day and burn it down the next!' to which I replied, 'If it had not been for me, it would not have been insured at all.'

James Dunwoody Bulloch   1862

Meanwhile the *Enrica* (*Alabama*) was taken into the Birkenhead Dock, where she was coaled and all her stores were put on board. Everything was kept in readiness for a start at short notice, but a full crew was not shipped, for fear that the men would be restive at the delay, and attract notice by their numbers and indiscreet talking.

In order to preserve due consistency in the order of events, it is now necessary to give an account of the arrangements for 'equipping' the *Alabama* – that is to say, the means adopted to supply that portion of her furniture which would complete her outfit as a vessel-of-war. It is not necessary to dwell long upon these arrangements. The battery was ordered very shortly after the contract for the ship was made, and all the ordnance supplies were put in train in good time; but such instructions were given as would ensure their being ready not much before the ship, although the parties contracted with were not informed for what purpose they were wanted, or even how they were to be shipped, until the time arrived for forwarding them. The necessary number of revolvers, short rifles with cutlass bayonets, ammunition, made-up clothing for 150 men, extra stores of all kinds, hammocks, and, in fact, everything required for the complete equipment of a man-of-war, were ordered, and instructions were given that the goods when ready should be packed, marked, and held for shipping orders.

Henry David Thoreau   1855

Is Heaven such a harbor as the Liverpool docks?

John Adamson 1817

2nd day the 29th

Our attention was now taken up with getting the luggage off the ship and passing the custom house with great diligence we compleated before the business closed – as the westerly winds had continued blowing for 8 or 10 days from 15 to 20 sail of vessels were got up this morning, all anxious to get into dock during todays high water, such confusion and clamour as I never before saw, people flocking to gase, with the ships crews, pilots and mates swearing and bawling out, was quite shocking. A large ship in her hurry run down a Welch sloop reducing her to a perfect wreck, and it was with great difficulty that they could get her into shoal water. JF having by this time got through which he proposed, we accordingly about 4 o'clock set out from Liverpool in the coach towards Manchester where we arrived at 9 o'clock in the evening and after seeing a few friends got to bed on still ground again.

William Palmer 1944

I would like to enthuse about the 1,575 mystic lights, which are recessed into the roof and sides of the Tunnel. There always seems to be a lurking mist in the depths which to

some eyes is silver, to others gold, to others just a shred of grey dust, the fumes of petrol and engine oils, which dims the distance, and the indirect illumination is intriguing. There is no shadow; the light is almost flat. The only colour seems to be the red flambeaux which are fire signals, and the green, red and amber sequence of traffic lights, where the Dock branches go off at Birkenhead and Liverpool.

Clive Barker   1956

Sometimes, of course, events uncover their mythic selves without any help from a writer. Such events often become part of our personal landscape; pivotal moments around which our lives seem to organize themselves. My first confrontation, in the flesh, with an image that had this kind of mythic resonance, occurred when I was very young. In May of 1956, as a four-year old, I was taken to an air show at Speke Airport, on the outskirts of Liverpool. It was a big event. The city was still getting out of its post-war doldrums, and entertainment was hard to come by. I have a very clear memory of what happened that day, a memory sharpened by the process of describing it in the drafts of this piece, and by several conversations with my father, who also plays a significant part in these events. I remember the heat of an intemperate day, and a tiny car filled with people. My parents; my aunt and uncle, my cousin, still a babe in arms. The air was stagnant, the sky blindingly bright. The family, lacking the wherewithal to get everyone inside the airfield so as to watch the fly-bys from the tarmac like the paying crowd, was parked at the edge of a cornfield close to the perimeter fence. I was bored, I think; the periods of waiting between the passing of the planes seemed interminable. My shirt stuck to the back of my neck; there were summer wasps buzzing around, coming after our sandwiches.

The high point of the afternoon's entertainment was to be a flight by a much-celebrated Bird Man. His name was Leo Valentin, and his performance, which had been seen throughout Europe (the man was French) was this: he jumped from a circling plane and glided on home-made balsa wood wings until he reached a certain altitude, at which point he pulled his rip-cord and parachuted to earth.

Our families waited through the heat of the afternoon for this last part of the show to begin, my father doing his best to interpret the words of the announcer on the airfield loudspeaker. Was that the Frenchman's plane: that tiny dark dot up there in the wide, empty sky? (This was the fifties; the sky was emptier then.) Yes, that was the plane, because look, there was Leo Valentin tumbling out, an even tinier dot. My uncle helped me follow him, explaining what I was seeing; but it didn't interest me very much. I was too hot and tired; too distracted by the wasps. And the spectacle, such as it was, seemed so remote, so undramatic. It required an adult's comprehension of the risks this man was taking to make the diminishing shape of the plane and Valentin's tumbling form seem significant.

I think my aunt began to panic first, her voice shrill. My uncle attempted to calm her, but her distress simply grew, as she watched the Bird Man descend.

Vaguely I began to understand what was happening. Something was wrong with the trick we were here to see. The man up there in the sky wasn't flying the way he was supposed to: *he was falling*.

Was there any concern being expressed by the voice on the

airfield loudspeaker? Perhaps; I don't remember. But I do remember the mounting panic of the adults, a panic not simply fuelled by the fact that Valentin was dropping out of the sky, but by their growing comprehension that he was going to hit the ground very close to us.

I think my mother must have taken me back to the car at this point. Certainly my next memory is the hot confines of the vehicle, and my mother instructing me not to look. This was a sight *I must not see*. You can imagine what a goad to my curiosity that was. Something was about to happen so terrible I was forbidden sight of it.

'*Don't look*,' my mother said, over and over. '*Don't look. Don't look. Don't look.*' My aunt was also in the car (perhaps she'd preceded us there) and my baby cousin was bawling in her arms.

In the confusion I defied my mother's repeated edict, and looked out towards the cornfield. My father and my uncle were standing at the edge of the field, their hands cupped over their brows to shield their eyes from the blazing sun, watching Leo Valentin plummet to his death.

(The image of a man falling out of the sky, his body and his ambitions dashed against the earth, is one that trails mythologies, of course. But it would be many years before I learned the story of Icarus, or read *Paradise Lost*. All I knew at that moment was the panic, and my hunger to see what the men out there were seeing; the thing I was forbidden.)

I was denied it, however. Probably my mother averted my eyes at the last minute, though it's unlikely I would have seen much. A blurred form dropping out of the blue, with the silk plume of a parachute following behind. It would have meant nothing.

My father, on the other hand, saw it all, and was one of the first to reach Valentin's body. I asked him about it, much, much later. He is a plain-spoken, pragmatic man, not given to waxing poetic, but when he answered my questions his vocabulary grew dreamy and evocative. The Bird Man's body, he said, had made a shape from the flattened grain, and he lay with his wings spread wide, so that it looked as though an enormous bird had fallen to earth. Of course they knew he was dead, but they turned him over anyway, I suppose to be absolutely sure. His face, my father told me, was not bloody, though a newspaper piece I later found about the accident speaks of 'severe head injuries'. His eyes were closed.

Perhaps, for completeness' sake, I should tell you how the tragedy came about. That flight, on May 21 1956, was to have been Leo Valentin's last; he'd been experimenting with the technology of unaided human flight since 1950, when he'd made his first jump at Villacoublay, and was now, at thirty-seven, ready to pursue a safer avenue of work. He was a superstitious man. He had asked for Room 123 at the hotel where he'd stayed (that was the number he called out before jumping); he would let no hands touch his wings but his own. Nobody is entirely certain what went wrong, but the favoured theory is that his wings clipped the plane as he jumped. He started to spin, and the damage to his wings prevented his controlling the descent. He attempted to open his parachute but it caught in the fractured wings, and candled.

Lorenza Stevens Berbineau 1851

July 21st Pleasent went shopping bought small leather bag gave five & sixpence english money bought some ribbon 17cts yard american money 62 cts they have some very nice shops. been packing for chester left in Liverpool my Carpet bag and Mrs Lowells sea things Miss Clink gone to London to day.

July 22nd We left Liverpool this morning for Chester we left the Adelphi house about 9 Oclock AM we went in a Cab to Monks ferry went on board of a small steam Boat which Carried us to Booking were we got out and went to the Rail way got into the Cars and went to Chester which is 15 miles from Liverpool we saw various Gardens with Hawthorn hedges nothing very beautiful the grass did not look as well as in America...

Charles Young 1835

A few minutes after 7 we started, not very fast at first, but, in less than five minutes, off we went like a shot from a gun. No sooner did we come to a field than it was a mile behind us, but this was nothing in comparison with meeting a long train of carriages from Liverpool. I was never so frightened in my life than at this moment; I shrank back completely horrified in my seat; I do not think the train was more than 2 seconds in passing, yet it was as long as Holywell Hill. We were then going at a full 34 miles an hour, consequently they passed us at double that time.

It is impossible to form any idea of the rapidity of moving. Several other trains passed us, but as I was aware of their approach they no longer alarmed me as at first. The first 17 miles we went in 32 minutes. I am much disappointed in the view of the country, the railway being cut through so many hills you have frequently for miles only clay mounds on each side of you – consequently no splendid prospect can attract your attention. Even when the railway is on a bridge or at an elevation above the usual track of land, you

are not charmed by that diversity of prospect which is to be met with in ordinary stage coach travelling. That has a decided superiority over this new work of man.

I was an hour and a quarter going the 33 miles, the latter part of the journey being performed at the slow speed of 20 miles an hour. Previous to entering Liverpool, you go through a dark, black, ugly, vile abominable tunnel of 300 yards long, which has all the horrors of banishment from life – such a hole as I never wish to go through again, unless my time is as precious as it was the other day.

John Hedges   1858

Monday 20 September 1858 We reached the Depot about 9 o,clock after a very long and tireing journey, the authorities very civil gave us some tea. Emigrants all gone on Board this morning. Had all the place to ourselves, very large, clean, & comfortless.

Tuesday 21 September 1858 – got up at 5 o clock, went

on board to see Farr found Mrs Farr with very bad cold, ship left the Depot while I was downstairs, had a difficult matter to get away from her had to climb down the side and scramble over a lot of boats and barges and scale, &c. Luggage came from station at $9^1/2$ a.m. it was too late when arrived last night to bring them. Had a walk in the Afternoon, to Birkenhead Park, it is very prettily laid out, it has an entrance very like the Marble arch, Hyde Park. The town is a miserable black looking affair, many of the Houses built of stone quarried on the spot, which is darkish coloured sandstone. I saw a Church, very lately finished, its color gave it a very singular appearance, the children run about the streets and in the Park (by scores), without shoes. They dry bricks here in a different way to whatever I saw before, they lay them flat all over the ground and when they are a little dry they are stacked in Hacks they are all slop made bricks and when they are picked up from the ground they pick a quantity of dirt with them which makes them very rough.

Wednesday 22 September 1858 – A very wet day thankfull that we had not to travel in it not allowed out today. passed the commissioners, received our Bags and repacked the Boxes we had opened, made already for going abroad several fresh Passengers came in, rather bad night on account of some comeing in late.

Thursday 23 September 1858 – went on Board this morning at ten o'clock, went in a steam tug several persons sick, but was better directly they were on board we had our arms examined by the surgeon to see if we had been vaccinated found our to be rather a disagreable berth next to the gang of Irish of which there seems a good many, had a fine moonlight view of Liverpool, the lamps reflected in the water had a very pretty effect; wife rather dull to day principally on account of our berth, received a letter from home to day and wrote an answer.

Arthur Ransome   1914

On the invitation of Professor Bernard Pares, I went to Liverpool University, where I was much encouraged over my Russian studies, and saw a magnificent sunset from the Mersey landing-stages.

Zangara   1849

We had now arrived nearly at the place of our destination (Liverpool). I will not attempt to describe my astonishment as we sailed up the river, and took our station in the docks, among hundreds of vessels, many of them larger than ours, which I had before considered as the wonder of the world. The immense buildings, and the perpetual bustle, almost bewildered my senses.

I knew not what was intended to be my lot, when almost every one was preparing to leave the ship; but before the lady before mentioned went, she came to me, accompanied by a gentleman who was come for her, the captain also being with them. She told me that it had been the captain's intention to have confined me below during his stay in port, but that she had engaged, in a penalty, for my not leaving the vessel, till I heard either from her or her husband, to whom she was going; that on my promising to do so, I might have my liberty in the vessel. This promise I readily made. The servant brought the child to take leave of me, and I was permitted to kiss it, as well as the lady's hand, which I did in tears.

I now took care to make myself as useful as I could on board, in assisting to unload the ship; and the captain and all the sailors were very kind to me. After a few days, the captain told me, that as he was sure I must want to see such a large and grand town, that I should that morning accompany him to several places to which he had to go. I certainly felt a great wish to do so, since it was probable I might never have another opportunity; but I recollected my promise to the lady, and told the captain that I dare not go. He looked at me attentively, and I thought I saw a tear; at last he condescended, before several of the men, to take my hand. 'You are a noble fellow,' said he; 'you are going into better hands, or I would have provided for you myself.' 'Here, sir,' said he to a gentleman whom I had not before noticed, but who had heard what had passed, 'take him, sir; I have had an eye to him during the whole voyage; and, if I know anything of mankind, he will be a faithful servant to you.' The gentleman now stepped up to me, shook me heartily by the hand, thanked me for saving the life of his child, and for my attention to his wife. He told me that I was then *free*, as he should send back the price of my freedom by the captain, and, therefore, I might go where I liked; but that, if I would go and live with him, it would give his wife much pleasure, and that he should make it his study to render me comfortable.

James Stonehouse 1863

Could we draw aside the thick veil of time that hides the future from us, we might perhaps behold our great seaport swelling into a metropolis, in size and importance, its suburbs creeping out to an undreamt of distance from its centre: or we might, reversing the picture, behold Liverpool by some unthought-of calamity – some fatal, unforeseen mischance, some concatenation of calamities – dwindled down to its former insignificance: its docks shipless, its warehouses in ruins, its streets grass-grown, and in its decay like some bye-gone cities of the east, that once sent out their vessels laden with 'cloth of blue, and red barbaric gold'. Under which of these two fates will Liverpool find its lot some centuries hence – which of these two pictures will it then present?

J B Priestley 1933

We reached the docks, put out our pipes and entered their precincts, where a vast amount of gloom and emptiness and decay was being carefully guarded. It was deep dusk. There were some last feeble gleams of sunset in the shadowy sky before us. Everything was shadowy now. The warehouses we passed seemed empty of everything but shadows. A few men – far too few – came straggling along, their day's work over. We arrived at the edge of the Mersey, and below us was a long mudbank. The water was a grey mystery, a mere vague thickening of space. Something hooted, to break a silence that immediately closed up afterwards to muffle the whole spectral scene. We walked slowly along the waterfront, from nothing, it seemed, into nothing; and darkness rose rather than fell; and with it came a twinkle of lights from Birkenhead that reached us not across the river but over a gulf that could not be measured. I have rarely seen anything more spectral and melancholy. It was hard to believe that by taking ship here you might eventually reach a place of sharp outlines, a place where colour burned and vibrated in the sunlight, that here was the gateway to the bronze ramparts of Arabia, to the temples and elephants of Ceylon, to flying fish and humming birds and hibiscus.

BIOGRAPHIES

John ADAMSON (1784-1857) was a Quaker wool merchant from West Yorkshire who took a six month business trip to America in 1817, leaving and returning via Liverpool packet ships.

Louisa May ALCOTT (1832-1888) sailed to Europe as a lady's companion in 1865, and used the short stay in Liverpool as the start of Amy's European tour in Part 2 of *Little Women* (published as *Good Wives* in the UK).

April ASHLEY (b 1935) was born George Jamieson in Norris Green in Liverpool, where as an effeminate young man she endured tough times, until in 1960 she became one of the first people to undergo sex reassignment surgery.

Dame Beryl BAINBRIDGE (b 1934) is a Lancashire-born novelist with more than twenty books to her name, some of which draw on her knowledge of Liverpool and time as an actress at the city's Playhouse Theatre.

Joseph BALLARD (1789-1877) was born into a Boston family who owned a livery and hack company, and sailed to Liverpool on business in 1815 through 'mountain waves.'

Clive BARKER (b 1952) was born in Liverpool, studied English and Philosophy at Liverpool University and now lives in California where he is a writer, film director and artist in the horror and urban fantasy genre.

Alan BENNETT (b 1934) is a Leeds-born playwright and actor who achieved instant fame at the 1960 Edinburgh Festival in the revue *Beyond the Fringe* and is now regarded as a national asset.

Lorenza Stevens BERBINEAU (d 1869) was a servant for a wealthy Boston family who sailed to Liverpool in 1851, en route to the Great Exhibition at London's Crystal Palace.

Isabella Lucy BIRD (1831-1904) was an explorer, mountaineer and travel writer who embarked from Liverpool on her first journey to America, and later became the first woman fellow of the Royal Geographical Society.

Sir James BISSET (1883-1967) was a Liverpool sea captain who was second officer on the SS *Carpathia* in April 1912 when it went to the aid of the stricken *Titanic*; he later became Commodore of the Cunard Line.

Fred BOWER (1871-1942) was born in America, raised in Liverpool and in 1904 left a Socialist manifesto beneath the foundation stone of the Anglican Cathedral where he was working as a stonemason.

Anne Tuttle Jones BULLARD (1808-1896) was an American author, published by the age of 22, who sailed to Europe with her clergyman husband in 1850 for the 3rd World

Peace Congress, arriving and leaving from Liverpool.

James Dunwoody BULLOCH (1823-1901) was a Confederate agent during the American Civil War who came to Liverpool in 1861 to assist the sailing of 'blockade runners' such as the *Alabama*.

Anthony BURGESS (1917-1993) was a novelist, linguist, composer and critic born in Manchester, most famous for his disturbing and prophetic novel *A Clockwork Orange*, and for his contempt of post-war pop culture.

Sir Richard BURTON (1821-1890) was an explorer and writer famous for his African travels, who took a post as British consul on Fernando Po, a small island off the coast of West Africa, leaving from Liverpool in 1861.

William CAMDEN (1551-1623) was born at the Old Bailey in London, and was a historian who travelled to Lancashire in 1582 to research *Britannia*, a topographical survey of Britain first published in Latin.

Thomas CATHER was a widely travelled Irishman who recorded his trip to America, sailing from Liverpool in February 1836 and returning to Ireland a year later, where he became a lawyer and later a Gaelic scholar.

Sir Edwin CHADWICK (1800-1890) was a government sanitary inspector who argued that disease and high mortality rates in cities such as Liverpool were directly related to living conditions.

Noam CHOMSKY (b 1928) is an American linguist and political philosopher known for his criticism of US foreign policy; he visited Liverpool in 2004 as part of the Writing on the Wall festival.

Thomas CLARKSON (1760-1846) was a relentless human rights campaigner who travelled 35,000 miles on horse-back around Britain, spending time in Liverpool gathering evidence against the slave trade but also about the treatment of sailors.

Carol COCHRANE was a Liverpool schoolgirl when she wrote about waiting for rehousing from an inner city area during the city's 'slum' clearances of the early 1970s.

Christopher COLBECK (1809-1838) was a pianoforte maker in London who started his journal aged 11 and described a thoroughly modern trip to Liverpool by train in 1831.

Samuel Taylor COLERIDGE (1772-1834) was a Romantic poet who 'spent a very pleasant week' in Liverpool in 1804 but moaned about the 'Lousy' Liverpool, the worst coach on the road.

William CRAFT (1824-1900) reached Liverpool in 1850 with his wife Ellen after a dramatic escape from slavery in Georgia, and spent two decades raising a family in London before returning to America in 1869.

Rosaria Delizia CROLLA (b 1978) was born in Glasgow to parents of Italian descent from the Lazio region; she came to Liverpool in 2004 and now runs the Italian Club café in Bold Street.

Samuel CURWEN (1715-1802) was a Massachusetts merchant who as a Loyalist during the American Revolution was exiled in England from 1775, returning in 1783 to find his business ruined.

Henry DAWSON was born in Deptford, London, was picked up as a 'waif and stray' by the Salvation Army, sent to the Olive Mount Children's Home in Liverpool and then to Canada at the age of 13, in 1913.

Thomas DE QUINCEY (1785-1859) spent three summers lodging at Everton, then a village on the shore near Liverpool, a decade before he became addicted to opium, and also returned in later years.

Samuel DERRICK (1724-1769) was a failed actor turned writer from Dublin who ended up as master of ceremonies at Bath and Tunbridge Wells, and whose published letters include descriptions of 'Leverpoole.'

Alexis DE TOCQUEVILLE (1805-1859) was a French aristocrat and social and political philosopher who became one of the first proponents of the new science of sociology;

he visited Liverpool briefly in 1835.

Charles DICKENS (1812-1870) was always warmly received in Liverpool, which he held 'second in his heart to London,' when he visited for his wildly popular public lectures.

Sir Edward ELGAR (1857-1934) was an English composer who conducted the premiere of his best known work, *Pomp and Circumstance March No.1*, at Liverpool's Philharmonic Hall in 1901.

Yvonne FOLEY (b 1946) was born in Liverpool and brought up in Toxteth and Kirkby, never knowing her natural father who was a Chinese seaman repatriated by the British Government after the Second World War.

Steven GERRARD (b 1980) is a footballer who was born in Huyton, Liverpool and joined Liverpool FC in 1998; he has played as the team captain since 2003 and made his England debut in 2000 against Ukraine.

William Ewart GLADSTONE (1809-1898) was born in Rodney Street, Liverpool into a religious family that also owned slave plantations, and became British prime minister no fewer than four times.

Ray GOSLING (b 1940) is a documenatry maker who was born in Chester and was a familiar face on Granada TV in the 1960s and 1970s, and for the offbeat series *Gosling's Travels*; his more recent programmes have championed the elderly.

Henry GREEN (1905-1973) was a novelist born into an upper class family who chose to work on the factory floor of the family firm in Birmingham, and portrayed working class life in his experimental novels.

Graham GREENE (1904-1991) was an introverted child who became one of the most revered writers of the twentieth century; his stay at the Adelphi and embarkation for Africa is chronicled in *Journey Without Maps*.

William Culshaw GREENHALGH witnessed the cruel treatment of the crew by the infamous Captain 'Bully' Forbes on his journey from Liverpool to Australia in 1853 aboard the *Marco Polo*, described in his vivid account of the journey.

James HANLEY (1901-1985) was a writer born in Dublin but brought up in Liverpool; his early stories were published in the *Liverpool Echo* and his uncomprosiming later novels portray an often brutal life at sea.

Nathaniel HAWTHORNE (1804-1864) was an American writer best known for *The Scarlett Letter*, who was US Consul to Liverpool from 1853-1857, living with his family in Rock Ferry on the Wirral.

John HEDGES (1828-1920) was a labourer from London who sailed in 1858 to Australia from Liverpool; his diary recounts how his first errand on reaching land was to bury his baby son, saying 'it is a sad beginning.'

Gerard Manley HOPKINS (1844-1889) was a poet and Jesuit priest sent to St Francis Xavier's parish in Liverpool, where he felt miserable, 'museless' and shocked by the poverty.

William Dean HOWELLS (1837-1920) was an American novelist and writer who wrote over a hundred books; he also served as US Consul to Venice in the 1860s, and on his return became an influential literary critic.

Elizabeth Pasto HUMMER (1912-2005) was born in Pennsylvania to Finnish parents weeks after they arrived in the US; the family had sailed from Liverpool because they had been unable to get tickets for the *Titanic*.

Carolyn IRVINE (b 1939) is a physiotherapist from Liverpool who now lives in Scotland, and is the great-great-granddaughter of Christopher Colbeck, whose diary is featured in Mersey Minis.

Washington IRVING (1783-1859) was the American author of *The Legend of Sleepy Hollow*, possibly written in Liverpool where he came in 1815 to work in the family hardware firm for several years.

Henry JAMES (1843-1916) was an American writer and novelist whose fictional characters often retrace his own steps through 'the dreadful delightful impressive streets' of Liverpool.

Derek JEWELL (1927-1985) was a jazz and pop music critic for the *Sunday Times* who visited Liverpool in 1963 to write about the new musical phenomenon and later documented its demise.

Frances Ann (Fanny) KEMBLE (1809-1893) was an actress born into a theatrical family in London whose eventful life included a trip on the opening day of the Liverpool to Manchester railway in 1830.

Reverend Francis KILVERT (1840-1879) was a Victorian clergyman whose now famously frank diaries weren't published until the late 1930s; only three volumes remain, the rest having been burnt by relatives.

Johann Georg KOHL (1808-1878) was a German geographer who visited Liverpool in 1844 to tour the docks and new industries, possibly to indulge in a bit of industrial espionage.

Sinclair LEWIS (1885-1951) was the first American to win the Nobel Prize for Literature and drew on his experiences working on cattleboats for his character Mr Wrenn who sails to Liverpool in 1910.

Malcolm LOWRY (1909-1957) was a novelist born in New Brighton, who took to both writing and alcohol at 15, went to sea at 18, and settled in Canada though he died in Sussex.

Jonathan MEADES (b 1947) is a British writer and broadcaster on art, architecture, food and culture whose acting training informs his idiosyncratic presenting style; he is also a member of the British Humanist Association.

George MELLY (1926-2007) led an unconventional life variously as art collector, TV critic, jazz singer, Surrealist and fisherman but was born into a respectable and well-connected Liverpool family.

Herman MELVILLE (1819-1891) was the American author of *Moby Dick*, first sailed to Liverpool as a cabin boy in 1839, and used the experience for his earlier novel *Redburn*.

John NEWTON (1725-1807) was a Liverpool slave trader whose spiritual journey exceeded all his seafaring when he experienced a religious conversion, became a clergyman and wrote the hymn *Amazing Grace*.

John OWEN (1878-1949) was the pseudonym of Liverpool-born novelist Frank Elias whose popular novels of the interwar years drew on his knowledge and love of Liverpool and Merseyside, though he had long moved to Suffolk.

William PALMER (1877-1954) was a writer born in Westmorland, son of a drover and grandson of a shepherd, who wrote topographical and travel books, including the first book to track the River Mersey from source to sea.

Richard PASSMORE (1920-1996) was born in Liverpool and joined the RAF at 17, survived the war but spent five years in captivity, and became a teacher and writer on his return to England.

Dean Edward PATEY (1915-2005) was the Anglican Dean of Liverpool from 1964 to 1982 who oversaw the completion of Liverpool Cathedral and became a popular church leader.

Henry 'Starbuck' PERRY was an American sailor interviewed about his life at sea, including being shanghaied in Liverpool, for the Federal Writers Project, which provided work for unemployed writers during the Depression.

Frederick Hawkins PIERCY (1830-1891) was an English artist commissioned by the Mormons to illustrate the 1853 emigration of a group of Latter-day Saints to Salt Lake City, Utah, via Liverpool.

Helen PITSILLOS (b 1968) was born in Liverpool into a Greek Cypriot family and was brought up in Toxteth and Belle Vale; she trained as a nurse and now lives in Scotland.

John Boynton PRIESTLEY (1894-1984) was a Bradford-born writer and founder member of CND whose travel writing from the 1930s, including a long passage about Liverpool, voices his social concerns.

Jonathan RABAN (b 1942) is an English travel writer and novelist whose modern-day sailing from the Liverpool docks, told in *Hunting Mr Heartbreak*, echoes the journeys of millions of emigrants to America.

Reverend Thomas RAFFLES (1788-1863) was born in London, moved to Liverpool in 1811 and was minister of the Great George Street Congregational Church, now known locally as 'the Blackie', for 49 years.

Arthur RANSOME (1884-1967) was a writer most famous for the children's book *Swallows and Amazons*; he also reported from Russia during the Bolshevik Revolution and married Trotsky's secretary.

Reverend James SHAW was an Irish Methodist who sailed to America in 1854 from Liverpool and whose spirited run-ins with 'infidels' on board the *Isaac Webb* are recounted in his travel book.

Benjamin SILLIMAN (1779-1864) was an American chemist and geologist, the first person to distill petroleum, who travelled to Edinburgh in 1805, landing and staying briefly in Liverpool.

Janet SMITH travelled as a lady's maid with her employers from Scotland via Liverpool to New York on the SS *Umbria* in September 1896, returning the following month unimpressed by America.

Fritz SPIEGL (1926-2003) was an Austrian musician and writer who arrived in England as a refugee in 1939; he was principal flute at the Royal Liverpool Philharmonic Orchestra from 1948-1963 and self-styled 'Scouseologist'.

James STONEHOUSE (c1809-1890) wrote memoirs of Liverpool life, reputedly as a local nonagenarian; in reality he was born in London, moved to Liverpool as a boy and remained until his death aged 81.

Henry David THOREAU (1817-1862) was an American author and philosopher sometimes cited as an inspiration to anarchists; he visited Liverpool only in his imagination, never having crossed the Atlantic.

Henry Theodore TUCKERMAN (1813-1871) was an American writer and essayist who cast a perceptive eye on the buildings, customs and commercial life of Victorian Liverpool during a visit to England in 1852.

Mark TWAIN (1835-1910) was perhaps America's most prolific and popular writer; he visited Liverpool on several occassions, and gave his only public lecture outside London in Liverpool in 1873.

Dirk Pieter VAN DEN BERGH (1864-1933) emigrated in 1906 from Holland to Canada with his wife Elske and nine children, writing in his diary about the stressful eight days' wait for a ship in Liverpool.

Jules VERNE (1828-1905) was a prolific and prophetic French writer who describes his departure for America from Liverpool in 1867 on the steamship *Great Eastern* in his novel *A Floating City*.

Sir Hugh WALPOLE (1884-1941) was a New Zealand-born writer who spent part of 1906 as a lay minister at the Mersey Mission to Seamen in Liverpool, before resolving to become a novelist.

Virginia WOOLF (1882-1941) was a novelist and feminist writer whose influential ideas shaped the modern novel; she travelled to Liverpool to sail on the maiden voyage of the *Anselm* in March 1905.

John WRAY emigrated with his family from Derby to America in 1818 and described the trouble the family had finding lodgings in Liverpool in his unpublished memoir.

Charles YOUNG was a traveller from Yorkshire who wrote to his sister Jane in August 1835 about his terrifying trip on the newly-built Liverpool to Manchester railway on his way to the Isle of Man.

ZANGARA was an African man who was taken to America some time in the 1840s by white slave traders from what is now Nigeria, and who escaped after several years of slavery aboard a Liverpool-bound ship in 1849, aged about 34 years.

BOOK LIST

John ADAMSON: *An Anglo-American traveller's diaries 1817, A Yorkshire Quaker Merchant's Journey by Sail, Steam and Stage*, ed Valda Swain, Autobus Review Publications, 1992

Louisa May ALCOTT: *Little Women, Vol 2*, Robert Brothers, 1869, published in UK as *Good Wives*, Ward, Lock & Tyler, 1880

April ASHLEY: *April Ashley's Odyssey*, Duncan Fallowell and April Ashley, Jonathan Cape, 1982

Beryl BAINBRIDGE: *English Journey*, Gerald Duckworth & Co, 1984

Joseph BALLARD: *England in 1815 As seen by a young Boston Merchant; being the reflections and comments of Joseph Ballard on a trip through Great Britain in the year of Waterloo*, Houghton Mifflin, 1913

Clive BARKER: *The Essential Clive Barker*, Harper Collins, 1999

Alan BENNETT: *Writing Home*, Faber & Faber, 1994

Lorenza Stevens BERBINEAU: *From Beacon Hill to Crystal Palace: The 1851 Travel Diary of a Working Class Woman*, ed Karen Kilcup, University of Iowa Press, 2002

Isabella Lucy BIRD: *The Englishwoman in America*, John

Murray, 1856

Sir James BISSET: *Tramps and Ladies, My Early Years in Steamers*, Angus and Robertson, 1960

Fred BOWER: *Rolling Stonemason*, Jonathan Cape, 1936

Anne Tuttle Jones BULLARD: *Sights and Scenes in Europe: A Series of Letters from England, France, Germany, Switzerland, and Italy, in 1850*, Chambers & Knapp, 1852

James Dunwoody BULLOCH: *The Secret Service of the Confederate States in Europe; or, How the Confederate Cruisers were Equipped*, Volume 1, Bentley and Son, 1883

Anthony BURGESS: *Little Wilson and Big God, Being the First Part of the Confessions of Anthony Burgess*, William Heinemann Ltd, 1987

Sir Richard BURTON: *Wanderings in West Africa, from Liverpool to Fernando Po*, Vol 1, Tinsley Brothers, 1863

William CAMDEN: *Camden's Britannia Vol II*, trs Edmund Gibson, London, 1772

Thomas CATHER: *Thomas Cather's Journal of a Voyage to America in 1836*, Rodale Press, 1955

Edwin CHADWICK: *Report from the Poor Law Commissioners on an Inquiry into the Sanitary Conditions of the Labouring Population of Great Britain*, London, 1842

Thomas CLARKSON: *The history of the rise, progress, and accomplishment of the abolition of the African slave-trade by the British Parliament*, Vol 1, London, 1808

Carol COCHRANE: *Our Street* from *This is your region: Liverpool & Merseyside*, Holmes McDougall, 1973

Christopher COLBECK: *The Journals of Christopher Colbeck, 1820-1837*, unpublished typescript held at Merseyside Maritime Museum Archives & Library

Samuel Taylor COLERIDGE: letter to the Morgans 11th February, 1812, from *Collected Letters of Samuel Taylor Coleridge*, ed Earl Leslie Griggs Vol III 1807-1814, Oxford: Clarendon Press, 1959

William CRAFT: *Running a Thousand Miles for Freedom; or, the Escape of William and Ellen Craft from Slavery*, William Tweedie, 1860

Samuel CURWEN: *The Journal of Samuel Curwen, Loyalist*, Volume 11, ed Andrew Oliver, Harvard University Press, 1972

Henry DAWSON: *My Memoirs*, unpublished typescript held at Merseyside Maritime Museum, DX/1434

Thomas DE QUINCEY: *On Murder Considered As One Of The Fine Arts* (Postcript in 1854), from *Tales and Prose Phantasies, The Collected Writings of Thomas De Quincey*, Volume XIII, ed David Masson, A & C Black, 1897

Samuel DERRICK: *Letters written from Leverpoole, Chester, Corke, the Lake of Killarney, etc*, L Davis & C. Reymers, London, 1767

Alexis DE TOCQUEVILLE: *Journeys to England and Ireland*, ed J P Mayer, trs George Lawrence & K P Mayer, Faber & Faber, 1958

Charles DICKENS: letter to Daniel Maclise, 3 January 1842, from *Letters of Charles Dickens, Vol III, 1842-1843*, ed Madeline House, Graham Storey, Kathleen Tillotson, Oxford: Clarendon Press, 1974

Steven GERRARD: from *Gerrard, My Autobiography*, Steven Gerrard and Henry Winter, Bantam Press, 2006

William Ewart GLADSTONE: from *The Life of William Ewart Gladstone, Vol 1 (1808-1859)*, John Morley, MacMillan & Co, 1903

Ray GOSLING: *Sum Total*, Faber & Faber, 1962

Henry GREEN: *Living*, The Hogarth Press, 1929

Graham GREENE: *Journey Without Maps*, Heinemann, 1936

William Culshaw GREENHALGH: *A Passenger's Diary written during a Passage to Australia in 1853 aboard the Marco Polo*, unpublished typescript held at Merseyside Maritime Museum, H2 Passage Narratives

James HANLEY: *Greaser Anderson*, from *The Last Voyage*, The Harvill Press, 1997

Nathaniel HAWTHORNE: *English Notebooks*, Kegan Paul, 1883

Gerard Manley HOPKINS: letter to Richard Watson Dixon, January 14, 1881, from *The Correspondence of Gerard Manley Hopkins and Richard Watson Dixon, 1844-1889*, Oxford University Press, 1963

John HEDGES: from a letter to his mother, September 1858, unpublished typescript held at Merseyside Maritime Museum, H2 Passage Narrative, DX/243

William Dean HOWELLS: *Seven English Cities*, Harper & Brothers, 1909

Washington IRVING: letter to Brevoort, 26 September, 1815, from *The Life and Letters of Washington Irving, by his nephew Pierre M. Irving. Vol 1*, G P Putnam, 1864

Henry JAMES: *The Ambassadors*, Methuen & Co, 1903

Derek JEWELL: from *The Popular Voice*, André Deutsch Ltd, 1980

Frances Ann KEMBLE: *Records of a Girlhood*, Richard Bentley & Son, 1878

Reverend Francis KILVERT: *Kilvert's Diary 1870-1879*, ed William Plomer, Penguin, 1938-40

Johann Georg KOHL: *In England and Wales, 1844*, Cass, 1968

Sinclair LEWIS: *Our Mr Wrenn, the Romantic Adventures of a Gentle Man*, Jonathan Cape, 1923

Malcolm LOWRY: *Ultramarine*, Jonathan Cape, 1933

George MELLY: *Revolt into Style*, Allen Lane, The Penguin Press, 1970

Herman MELVILLE: *Redburn, His first voyage*, 1849

John NEWTON: letter to his wife, August 1754, from *History of the Liverpool Privateers and Letters of Marque, with an account of the Liverpool Slave Trade 1744-1812*, Gomer Williams, Heinemann, 1897, Liverpool University Press, 2004

John OWEN: *The Cotton Broker*, Hodder & Stoughton, 1921

William PALMER: *The River Mersey*, Robert Hale Ltd, 1944

Richard PASSMORE: *Thursday is Missing*, Thomas Harmsworth, 1984

Edward PATEY: *My Liverpool Life*, Mowbray, 1983

Frederick Hawkins PIERCY: *Route from Liverpool to Great Salt Lake City*, ed Fawn M Brodie, Belknap Press of Harvard University Press, 1962

J B PRIESTLEY: *English Journey*, Heinemann, 1934

Jonathan RABAN: *Hunting Mr Heartbreak*, Collins Harvill, 1990

Reverend Thomas RAFFLES: from letter to his father, *Memoirs of the Life and Ministry of Thomas Raffles*, Sir Thomas Stamford Raffles, 1864

Arthur RANSOME: *The Autobiography of Arthur Ransome*, ed Rupert Hart-Davis, Jonathan Cape, 1976

Reverend James SHAW: *Twelve Years in America: Being the Observations on the Country, the People, Institutions and Religion; with Notices of Slavery and the Late War*, Hamilton, Adams and Co., 1867

Benjamin SILLIMAN: *A Journal of Travels in England, Holland and Scotland, and of Two Passages over the Atlantic, in the Years 1805 and 1806, Vol 1*, Howe & Deforest, and Increase Cook & Co, 1810

Janet SMITH: *Diary of a lady's maid, 1896*, unpublished typescript held at Merseyside Maritime Museum, H2 Passage Narratives

James STONEHOUSE: *Recollections of Old Liverpool by a nonagenarian*, J F Hughes, 1863

Henry David THOREAU: *Cape Cod*, Houghton, Mifflin & Co., 1865

Henry Theodore TUCKERMAN: *A Month in England*, Redfield, 1853

Mark TWAIN: letter to Dr John Brown from the Washington Hotel, Lime Street, Aug 1879, from *Mark Twain's Letters, Arranged with Comment by Albert Bigelow Paine, Vol III*, Harper, 1917

Dirk Pieter VAN DEN BERGH: unpublished diary held at Merseyside Maritime Museum Archives & Library,

Jules VERNE: *A Floating City, 1874*, Sampson Low, Marston, Low and Searle

Hugh WALPOLE: *The Crystal Box*, 1924, from Hugh Walpole, Rupert Hart-Davis, Macmillan, 1952

Virginia WOOLF: *A Passionate Apprentice, The Early Journals of Virginia Woolf*, ed Mitchell A Leaska, The Hogarth Press, 1990

Henry WRAY: *Wray family memoirs*, unpublished typescript held at Merseyside Maritime Museum, DX/562

Charles YOUNG: letter to his sister Jane, August 1835, from *A Book of Railway Journeys*, Ludovic Kennedy, Rawson, Wade Publishers, 1980

ZANGARA: *Slavery Illustrated In the Histories of Zangara and Maquama, Two Negroes Stolen from Africa and Sold into Slavery Related by Themselves*, Simpkin, Marshall and Co, 1849

ACKNOWLEDGEMENTS

John Adamson, *An Anglo-American Traveller's Diaries, 1817*: reproduced by kind permission of Autobus Review Publications

April Ashley, *April Ashley's Odyssey* © Duncan Fallowell and April Ashley, Jonathan Cape, 1982: by kind permission of Duncan Fallowell and April Ashley

Beryl Bainbridge, *English Journey*: reprinted by kind permission of Gerald Duckworth & Co Ltd © Beryl Bainbridge 1984

Clive Barker, *The Essential Clive Barker*: reprinted by permission of HarperCollins Publishers Ltd. © Clive Barker 1999

Alan Bennett, *Writing Home:* by permission of Faber and Faber Ltd

Lorenza Stevens Berbineau, *From Beacon Hill to Crystal Palace*: published by the University of Iowa Press

James Bisset, *Tramps and Steamers: My Early Years in Steamers* by Sir James Bisset and P.R. Stephensen: reprinted by kind permission of HarperCollins Publishers Ltd.

Fred Bower, *Rolling Stonemason*: published by Jonathan Cape. Reprinted by permission of The Random House Group Ltd.

Anthony Burgess, from *Little Wilson and Big God*, by Anthony Burgess, published by William Heinemann: reprinted by permission of The Random House Group Ltd.

Thomas Cather, *Journal of a Voyage to America in 1836*: by permission of Rodale Press

Noam Chomsky: by kind permission of Noam Chomsky and Mathew Capper, private correspondence, 2007

Christopher Colbeck, *The Journals of Christopher Colbeck, 1820-1837*: reproduced by kind permission of Joyce Colbeck Robinson and family

Samuel Taylor Coleridge, *Collected Letters of Samuel Taylor Coleridge*: reproduced by kind permission of Oxford University Press

Samuel Curwen, *The Journal of Samuel Curwen, Loyalist, Volume 11*: Reprinted by permission of the publishers from THE JOURNAL OF SAMUEL CURWEN, LOYALIST, edited by Andrew Oliver, pp. 627-628, Cambridge, Mass: Harvard University Press, Copyright © 1972 by the Essex Institute

Henry Dawson, *My Memoirs*: reproduced courtesy of National Museums Liverpool (Merseyside Maritime Museum)

Charles Dickens, *letter to Daniel Maclise, 3 January 1842*, from *Letters of Charles Dickens, Vol III, 1842-1843*, ed by Graham Storey & Kathleen Tillotson (1974): reproduced by kind permission of Oxford University Press

Edward Elgar, from a letter from Sir Edward Elgar to H. Ernest Roberts, 2 Jul 1924: by kind permission of the Rodewald Concert Society

Yvonne Foley: by kind permission of 800 Lives Contemporary Collecting Project, Museum of Liverpool, National Museums Liverpool

Steven Gerrard, from Dedication in *Gerrard: An Autobiography* by Steven Gerrard, published by Bantam Press: reprinted by permission of The Random House Group Ltd

Ray Gosling, *Sum Total* (Faber & Faber 1962): reproduced by kind

reproduced by permission of PFD (www.pfd.co.uk) on behalf of the Estate of J.B. Priestley

Jonathan Raban, *Hunting Mister Heartbreak*: published by Harvill: reprinted by permission of The Random House Group Ltd.

Arthur Ransome, *The Autobiography of Arthur Ransome,* published by Jonathan Cape: reprinted by permission of The Random House Group Ltd.

Janet Smith, *Diary of a lady's maid, 1896*: reproduced courtesy of National Museums Liverpool (Merseyside Maritime Museum)

Fritz Spiegl: by kind permission of Ingrid Spiegl

Dirk Pieter Van Den Bergh: reproduced courtesy of National Museums Liverpool (Merseyside Maritime Museum)

Hugh Walpole: by kind permission of Duff Hart-Davis

Virginia Woolf, *A Passionate Apprentice*: published by Hogarth Press. Used by permission of the executors of the Virginia Woolf Estate and The Random House Group Ltd

Henry Wray, *Wray family memoir*: reproduced courtesy of National Museums Liverpool (Merseyside Maritime Museum)

We have gone to great lengths to get permission to reproduce every work still in copyright, but in a few cases it has proved impossible to trace the copyright holders.

ILLUSTRATIONS

These striking illustrations were commissioned for Mersey Minis from artist Clare Curtis, and present her unique visual response to Liverpool. Clare follows a long tradition of British printmakers with her distinctive linocuts, which are imbued with a bold, contemporary feel. Felixstowe-based Clare demonstrates her empathy with the sea with maritime patterns and motifs appearing throughout her work. These images have been chosen for their multi-layered local references.

These illustrations and all five covers are available as prints – for details, go to the website at www.merseyminis.com

Taxi: The famous shape of the black cab is seen in few cities outside London. Taxis can be found in Liverpool's various gateways for travellers and commuters, as well as carrying exhausted revellers home at weekends.

Block and tackle: The distinctive patterns of ropes, hooks, chains and pulleys are strongly associated with shipping and construction and symbolise departure, whether from the past or from the place.

Eros: Sculptor Sir Alfred Gilbert insisted that his famous fountain depicted Anteros, symbol of philanthropic love, and not his lustful twin Eros. Liverpool's fountain is in the leafy surroundings of Sefton Park.

Football: The city's passion for football is a partisan story of triumphs and tragedies. Amongst the long list of Merseyside football firsts is the brilliant city engineer John Brodie's invention of football nets.

Liver Bird: Originally the Eagle of St John the Divine, the bird evolved after the Civil War into Liverpool's mythical guardian, carrying a bit of seaweed rather than Plantagenet King John's symbol of *planta genista*, or broom.

Pub sign: Representing not only a favoured pastime of locals and visitors alike, we have chosen not only a famous city centre pub, but a historic shipping name with strongly emotional associations.

Palm House: The Sefton Park Palm House was opened in 1896 by Queen Victoria. Smashed first by the Blitz in 1941, then later by neglect, it was restored to its former splendour and reopened in 2001.

Front door: Georgian doors, with their distinctive fanlights, can still be seen in areas of Liverpool such as Everton, Canning, and Ropewalks. These were the homes of Liverpool's 18th century merchants.

Trunk: Liverpool has always been a city on the move; thousands of travellers pass every month through the port, the airport and Lime Street Station, braced for a new life with their worldly possessions.

Capstan and rope: For centuries people came to and left Liverpool by sea; these are evocative symbols of arrival and departure, also resonating with the city centre's Rope Walks district.

Steam train: Stephenson won the Rainhill Trials with *Rocket* in 1829, for the world's first passenger railway line (Liverpool to Manchester); classic toys Hornby Trains and Meccano were invented in Liverpool.

Cotton: Bound up with the city's fortunes – cotton picked by slaves transported by Liverpool ships, trade links with India and Egypt; even today 70% of world cotton for export is sold under Liverpool arbitration.

Music: Liverpool boasts world-class music from sea shanties to the Royal Liverpool Philharmonic; Merseybeat hit international consciousness in the 1960s, but owes its heritage to cultures from around the world.

Neptune: Roman God of the Sea, mythical feature on the city coat of arms; the planet Neptune was the final home of the highly evolved human race in local writer Olaf Stapledon's *Last and First Men*.

Oak leaves: Quintessentially English; the Allerton Oak (over 1,000 years old); timber exports from Liverpool; the district of Aigburth means 'grove of oaks'; oak timbers were used to build ships on the Mersey.

THE EDITOR

Though a land-lubber herself, Deborah Mulhearn was born in Liverpool into a family with a typically seafaring tradition.

She left school at 16 and worked in the wardrobe department of the Liverpool Playhouse. She then went back to formal education, studying English Literature at the University of Liverpool.

After the requisite stint in London, where she worked for five years in publishing and as a journalist on the Architects' Journal, she returned to Liverpool in 1991 to pursue a freelance career in journalism. She writes for a wide variety of newspapers and magazines and has contributed to several books on architecture, history and environment.

THANKS

Grateful thanks for multifarious help and support with LEAVING to: Michael Bailey; Sakina & Neil Burgess; Mathew Capper; Katherine Constable; Rosaria Crolla; Mary Earnshaw; Paul Gallagher, Museum of Liverpool; Roger Hull, Liverpool archives and local studies; David & Carolyn Irvine; Adrian Jarvis; Karen Kilcup, University of North Carolina; Vince McKernan, Royal Liverpool Philharmonic Archives; Rachel Mulhearn, Merseyside Maritime Museum; Tim

Nicholas, Cambridge University Library; Helen Mulhearn; Andy Sawyer and staff at Special Collections and Archives, Sydney Jones Library, University of Liverpool; Deborah & David Singmaster; Humphrey Southall, Great Britain Historical GIS Project, University of Portsmouth; Ingrid Spiegl; Beccy Turner, Wordsworth Trust; David Wright, Wisbech and Fenland Museum.

LEAVING and the whole of Mersey Minis has been essentially a massive research project, and a fair number of the extracts are here thanks to the knowledge and generosity of many people. There are writers included who I'd never heard of, and others who I had no idea had been to Liverpool.

I'd also like to thank everyone who helped in different ways on Mersey Minis: Ken Ashcroft; Michael Bhaskar; Leslie Boss; Polly Byrne; Gladys-Mary Coles, editor, *Both Sides of the River*; Jamie Cowen; Jane Cramb; Amy de Joia, David Fleming, National Museums Liverpool; Terri Harding; Andrew Hewson; Ben Kennedy; Joanne Lampen; Elaine Maruhn; Pauline McAdam, BBC Radio Merseyside; Helena McConnell; Mike Neary; Jenny Needham; David Robinson; Helen Threlfall; Catherine Trippett; Adam Turner and many others.

Particular thanks to Arabella McIntyre-Brown and Fiona Shaw of Capsica who took the leap of faith to publish Mersey Minis and to illustrator Clare Curtis who expertly expressed the themes and ideas.

Thanks also to my family and friends who listened and laughed throughout and to my daughter Beth who had no choice but to live with Mersey Minis for the two years I worked on the series, and did so with grace and humour.

INDEX OF AUTHORS

MERSEY MINIS

LEAVING is the fifth and final volume in the Mersey Minis series, published during 2007, Liverpool's 800th anniversary year. Four volumes – LANDING, LIVING, LOVING, LEAVING – are collections of writing from the past eight centuries. The third volume in the series, LONGING, contains entirely new writing from around the world, marking a beat in Liverpool's remarkable  history (this volume is not available to buy separately, as it was an anniversary gift to the city on 28 August 2007).

However, the series of five volumes is now available as a boxed set; for details, log on to www.merseyminis.com

CAPSICA

Capsica is an independent publishing house based in Liverpool, specialising in high quality non-fiction. If you have enjoyed LEAVING, you might like to see some of our other publications. You can read about the books on their blogs, and buy on www.loveliverpoolbooks.com.

http://liverpoolfirst1000years.blogspot.com
http://cultureofcapital.blogspot.com/
http://napkinfolding.blogspot.com/